# A VERY BRITISH LESBIAN

Be sure to catch Fiona Goodwin's one-woman show. It's hilariously honest and refreshingly authentic. The book "had me laughing out loud and wanting more."

—Drew Heriot
Director of the *The Secret*

Few have the ability to combine comedy and pathos, to walk that fine line between laughter and tears. I saw such a rare gifted performer last week in a sold out theatre performance in Santa Monica, CA, Fiona Goodwin is 'a very British lesbian.' For one hour, she took us through a journey of the struggle between her religious upbringing and her attraction toward women. She delivers her story so brilliantly, that the audience goes through her life's ups and downs, laughing all the way. By the end, I wanted to jump up on stage and hug her, for having gone through so much to just 'come out,' but the standing ovation lasted too long.

This woman, who grew up in the very proper British countryside, has created a phenomenal show that is not to be missed.

—Robin Tyler
Called the 'mother of gay comedy,' Robin was the first out lesbian or gay comic on TV. Her 1979 album *Always a Bridesmaid, Never a Groom* is now in the Smithsonian.

"Fiona delivers her soul-baring tale with such comic dexterity and deftness, that she gifts the audience with something quite precious and contradictory; the power to see each painful step in her journey with compassion and empathy, giving sweet permission to have a hearty laugh at it all."

—Russell Carpenter
Oscar-Winning Cinematographer, *Titanic*

It is a wonderful thing to sit in the dark and let really good writing delight you. **This is not just good, it is writing of such skill and precision that it could have been done with a diamond cutter.** There is not one single wasted word, not one phrase that does not play perfectly—and sometimes painfully—its part in this extraordinary story of love and life, fear and finding yourself.

Even with the staging, the simplistic illustrations used deflect the emotions of the situations they portray just enough to prick but not stab your feelings.

There is no actual imperative to be lesbian (or even lesbian-ish) to be enthralled, although it helps. Fiona Goodwin—for the Very British Lesbian, 'tis she—takes us, by the heart, though a childhood and teenage so mired in guilt and confusion that she became a Born Again Christian and ended up being exorcised by a gangster pastor and a woman with elephantitis. Years of denial (and therapy) led to decades in the closet (and therapy), interspersed with a series of doomed love affairs with variously unavailable women.

And one non-love affair with a too-available man. Goodwin perfectly matches the writing **with an exquisitely nuanced, pared-back performance.**

It is, as mentioned in the title, all Very British. But her lesbian heart in hiding left her endlessly running away, across the world—to Italy and Honduras, London and L.A—trying to avoid Mz Right and consequently meeting several Mz Wonderful But Ultimately Wrong.

**There is so much laughter in Goodwin's hour** that it is a tribute to her as both writer and performer that it does not for one second diminish the hurt that is felt, it simply refuses to let things get either angry or maudlin.

Which makes this **a memorably powerful hour.** And very British.

—Kate Copstick
★★★★★ *The Scotsman*, Edinburgh Festival 2019

# A VERY BRITISH LESBIAN

## FIONA GOODWIN

LUMINARE PRESS

WWW.LUMINAREPRESS.COM

Luminare Press
442 Charnelton St.
Eugene, OR 97401
www.luminarepress.com

LCCN: 2021918723
ISBN: 978-1-64388-735-7

*This book is a rallying cry for anyone*
*who aspires to live out loud.*

With love,

Fiona xx

Provincetown Oct 21

With love,

# CHAPTER ONE

My name is Fiona Goodwin and I am a very British lesbian. It took me four seconds to write that sentence and forty years to know it, and then own it.

My first kiss was an accident.

I was eighteen. We were sharing a single bed for financial reasons. Lydia worked the nightshift at the hospital and that gave me the bed to myself most nights. When she wasn't working, we squashed together. It bothered me how much I looked forward to that. On this particular chilly November morning, my heart pounded especially hard as I felt the worn covers of the metal sprung bed being pulled back. It was 6.30 a.m. She climbed in. I felt her weariness at the end of a long night. I feigned sleep, jamming myself against the wall. She adjusted her thick flannel nightie and lay still. Silence descended and just when I thought she had settled, got comfy, she placed her ice-cold foot on the back of my bare leg,

"Ouch!" I yelled, "you're freezing!" I spun around to face her, "Keep your feet on your own side!" She burst into giggles. By the light of the city street lamps, I could make out her crinkled laughing eyes, the long black messy curls against pale English skin. I grabbed her wrists and we tussled till she was close to falling out of the bed.

Spluttering she begged, "Okay! I give in!"

"Say you're sorry!" I demanded.

"I'm sorry!" She was still giggling.

"You are a cheeky young lady!" I declared, and in my bossiest voice, "On this occasion I will forgive you!"

Like playful children, we hugged and made up. Then we pulled back. Breathless, smiling, we held each other's gaze, our faces almost touching. Her hair tickled my nose. The laughing subsided, there was just stillness. And a longing, a longing for what I didn't know. I moved in closer. What was I doing?! I put my lips gently on hers and she didn't pull away. I felt intoxicated, dizzy. I wanted to stay there. Feeling awkward and being British I suppose, I turned and faced the other way. Away from her. She was awake, I was awake, we just lay there. Nothing was said.

The next morning, without waking her, I crept out of bed and phoned Mick, he was the pastor of the fundamentalist charismatic house church that I attended. I told him I needed to talk. It was serious. He suggested I come straight away. I chained my bike to the railings at Kings Cross Station and took the 274 bus up to Regents Park. I had never kissed a girl. I would tell Mick and he might know if God could help me. The red double-decker bus took about twenty minutes and dropped me right outside their four-story regency home on a busy Camden Rd. I felt sick with fear. I let the bus come to a complete standstill before swinging around the pole at the back and lowering myself down. When a gap appeared in the traffic, I trotted across the road and up the worn stone steps to the front door. I hesitated to press the doorbell, something I had happily done many times before. My stomach was churning. There was always a hug waiting for me here, a sense of belonging. Mick and his wife Pauline were in their late fifties, cockney through and through. They had two perfect teenage daughters who wore A-line skirts and had long black Christian hair. Their dress was modest, no cleavage and very big Bibles—well-worn and always on their person. Mick and Pauline had kind, lined faces. They laughed a lot. They were the salt of the earth. We university students were far from home and grateful for the extended family. For me especially, these two dear souls were the warmth and consistency that I had not found with my own parents. Mick was bald and short, Pauline cuddly and short. Her right leg was twice the width of her left leg—she had elephantitis.

Mick constantly pointed out the irony, that here he was, a man without education, shepherding these "posh University of London brainiacs" as he put it. His honesty about how out of place he felt was endearing. He was humble, so was Pauline, both of them delighted to serve the student community. They embraced the fact that this is where God had placed them.

"Him up there's got a sense of humour, eh?!" Mick would joke.

At their door, I was motionless, gripped with fear. How would they respond? How would I even say it? I wondered if I would be allowed to stay in the church. I had never met a lesbian. I hated the word. The worst insult at school was lesbo. "You a lesbo or something?!" In the 1980s were no lesbians on television, just camp homosexual men and they were the brunt of all their own jokes.

I finally pressed my index finger firmly on the gold-plated bell. There was no going back. I heard Mick clumping down the stairs. He appeared, chuckling as he swung wide the heavy blue door, "Hello, love! Come on in." He gave me a big bear hug and I followed him up the stairs.

"Pauline's put the kettle on," he winked.

The sitting room was on the second floor, with chunky upholstered armchairs and a long green shabby sofa. Plates from English seaside towns were displayed on the walls. I've never understood plates on walls. Pauline appeared with a colourful metal tea tray. It had on it an image of the beach at Brighton. Her leg was huge today. She never complained.

Mick, never one to mince his words, got right to the point, "So what's this all about, Claire? 'Ow can we 'elp?"

He asked so sincerely. I would have to tell him something that merited the inconvenience of this impromptu visit. But the words weren't coming. I remembered how much I didn't want to be attracted to girls, that I had kissed Lydia, that I was in love and knew I couldn't be. The Bible forbade it. The church forbade it. My mother spoke of those "unnatural people" in hushed tones. How pitiful, I wanted to be an international healer, bringing liberation to the lost. The shame, the possibility that I could be a lesbian, was a far cry from the glorious international ministry that I had envisioned for myself.

I blurted out, "I've kissed Lydia."

Mick looked nonplussed, "What's wrong with that then?"

I was blushing now. "I mean I *kissed* Lydia."

"You what? You *kissed* her kissed her?" His voice had lowered. His speech more deliberate.

Pauline fiddled with the hem of her plaid wool skirt. She seemed to wince. Mick looked equally uncomfortable. They sank deeper into their armchairs. I was hunched over on the squishy green sofa.

"Go on," he said. Normally he would have made a joke by now.

I struggled on, "Well, I've had boyfriends and it's not that I don't like boys but something happened last night..."

*Fiona Goodwin*

Silence.

Awkward caring stares.

"I've always had terrible crushes on girls but it's the first time I've kissed one. At school I used to stalk them, I would hide in the bushes at the bus stop. Sometimes I would get on the wrong bus just so I could…"

Mick gestured to stop. "All right love, I've got the picture. We better 'ave that cuppa tea. Pauline?" He nodded to her to pour.

The clinking of cups was followed by quiet sipping, thinking time it felt like. Mick swallowed. I was starting to feel concerned for them.

"So you kissed Lydia?" he said.

"Yes," I said, and then defensively, "and she kissed me back."

I hadn't planned on saying that because I didn't want to incriminate her. It just came out. After all, I was the one with the problem. It wasn't her fault.

"You mean Lydia Watson?" he asked. His gilt-edged porcelain china teacup clattered a little too loudly on the saucer.

"No," I stuttered, "Lydia Bronson." Why was he even asking me that? There were two Lydia's at church. There was my Lydia and then there was Lydia Watson who had three grandchildren and owned a horse racing stable. Why would he think it was Lydia Watson? That bothered me. He actually thinks I would kiss Lydia Watson? She's in her sixties and married. What does he take me for? It bothered me that he put me and Lydia Watson together. And then I thought, what difference did it make which Lydia I had kissed. Suddenly I wanted to cry. Tears welled up and crept over my cheeks. Wiping them away felt pointless. I wanted to say how extraordinary it felt to kiss Lydia Bronson, how sweet she was and how there wouldn't feel any point to life without her.

What was Jesus thinking? Making me love this beautiful, generous soul? It felt cruel. I didn't care anymore about my so-called international ministry and saving souls. Was it wrong for me to love Lydia as much as I did, like it was wrong for me to love Jane, and Caroline and Samantha and God knows who else? A motherly shoulder to cry on would have been useful at this point. I could feel how having someone to put their arms around me, the way that Lydia had the night before, would have really helped.

Pauline was now topping up the teacups with milk. When she looked up at me, her eyelids fluttered and her reassuring smile required a little too much effort.

"She's terrified," I thought.

I was suddenly worried for Lydia. "I don't want to get Lydia in trouble," I pleaded.

"Don't worry, Claire," Mick said. "We will talk to Lydia. She's not in trouble but it would be best that you stay away from her from now on."

I nodded.

Stay away from her? Lydia was my best friend. The indescribable chasm that opened up in me when those words were spoken was the violence and desolation of Dante's second circle of hell. Dante's Inferno was my area of expertise—I was a student of Italian and French. The punishment in the second circle was to be blown violently, back and forth by strong winds, preventing the sufferers eternally from finding peace and rest. Cleopatra was in the second circle of hell. She would never find rest because she loved Anthony too much. He was in hell because he had deserted the battlefield to be with her. I hoped that they at least were being buffeted about together. I loved that story, lovers failing in their duties because of their love for each other.

Mick pulled himself up straight, cheeks slightly pink, but he sounded confident, "I know what we'll do. We'll get Uncle Ern up from Cornwall, 'e'll know what to do. You see Claire, you 'ave a demon and Uncle Ern, 'ee knows 'ow to get 'em out."

A demon? Being possessed had not been my first thought, but on a positive note, Mick was saying that a demon could be got rid of, whereas a psychological sickness was more of a challenge.

"So you can get the demon out?" I inquired.

"Yes, but you really 'ave to want to. The 'omosexual demon don't come out that easy. Other demons, you can exorcise no problem."

"Exorcise?" I shuddered at the sound of that. But on the other hand, Mick's matter-of-fact tone made it seem very doable. Also, I admired Uncle Ern (short for Ernest,} the seventy-year-old overseer of our church. His empathy and insight had reduced me to tears more than once. Mick whispered to Pauline, not loudly enough, "A return ticket from Cornwall will be eighty pounds." He saw my worried face and quickly added, "Don't worry love, the church will pay for it."

This was embarrassing. Our ten percent tithes were meant to pay for the building and to support Mick's family, as well as the outreach project to the homeless. It wasn't meant for exorcising demons! But if they could get the demon out then I would be less tormented and more useful and Lydia and I could continue to team up on the home-less project.

"Go 'ome Claire, don't eat nuffink for three days and come back Saturday. Whatever you do, stay right away from Lydia."

"Thanks, Mick." I pushed myself up out of the comfy armchair and he gave me a hug. It felt good to have let it all out and for there to be a solution. Pauline returned the tea tray to the kitchen and came back to engulf me in her kind arms. I wondered if it worried her and if she felt okay to touch me, her being a woman. And wouldn't they be worried about hugging someone with a demon? I went down the stairs and let myself out into the warm midday sun. Is this how hope felt? I wondered how I would feel about Lydia with the demon gone and would I ever feel that kind of love again. I wanted to talk to her and reassure her that it would all be okay and that I wasn't rejecting her, but out of nowhere I fell back into the chasm, the bleakest feeling of belonging nowhere, to no one. Hopefully, this would be temporary. I got fish and chips on the way home. I ate it on the step outside the flat because one of my flat-mates, Helen, didn't like the lingering smell of fish.

# CHAPTER TWO

That Thursday evening at church, Lydia visibly turned her back on me. She had big rings under her eyes as if she had been crying. God forgive me! Look what I've done! I should never have made friends with her. She didn't deserve this. She chatted breezily with Michael, who worked at the BBC. It was a body blow, a sword to the heart. I wanted to say sorry, sorry for what had happened, sorry for speaking up. It all felt sordid and horrid but that was who I was and I couldn't pretend otherwise. Life had been fun with Lydia and now it was empty. I wondered what had been said and if she felt betrayed. I was doing it for her as much as for me. I had seen how much she loved me and I didn't want to lead her down the wrong path. I went and drank my tea with the children from the homeless project who were stuffing pink wafer biscuits into their pockets. Mick's message that week was about Jesus walking on the water and Peter stepping out of the boat to meet him. Peter got scared and started to sink. Jesus saved him, then rebuked him, "Oh ye of little faith, why did you doubt me?"

I tried to find a message for myself but I was frozen. Sinking for sure. Missing Lydia terribly.

I got a phone call the next day from Mick giving me a time to come for the exorcism. "Come at ten. You remember only water for three days? Uncle Ern says that this one's a bit of bugger to get out and fasting loosens its hold."

That made sense: starve it out. I was already so hungry. Not eating focused my mind very much on the seriousness of my condition. I had heard of people having prayer for all sorts of things but no one had ever had to fast for three days. The more miserable I became, the more sure I was that this was going to be the answer. I looked forward to not falling in love with all my friends and then losing them for that same reason. It would be a whole new life. I paced the beige hessian carpet in the flat, feeling the roughness under my bare feet. Helen knew that I had a "mystery condition" that was bringing the much loved and revered Uncle Ern up from Cornwall.

"Wow," she said, "You're so lucky, I wish I could get that kind of help." Her subtext was, "Wow, it must be really bad for Uncle Ern to come up."

I did feel special. Uncle Ern was renowned for his spiritual insight. A married friend in the church had been having an affair, Uncle Ern edged up to her, took her hand and without any prior knowledge whispered in her ear, "You need to let go of him m'lover, Jesus loves you and you know that your children need you."

This was what was called a "word of knowledge," one of the gifts of the Holy Spirit. She burst into tears and sobbed in his arms. He said nothing more, patted her on the head, and winked. She subsequently ended the affair and became the poster child for fidelity. She testified in church to whoops and cheers and a standing ovation. I wondered if I could ever get that same response. I didn't think so somehow but I desperately wanted to be able to testify like her and get a standing ovation. Maybe I would become the poster child for ex-homosexuals?

*Fiona Goodwin*

During my fasting that week, and in between praying in tongues, I watched the Spurs-Manchester soccer match and cried when Bobby Charlton scored. The crowd roared as he was hoisted onto the shoulders of his teammates. That must be amazing, being up there and being cheered on. My own football career had ended at age eleven when it was decided that I could not play on the school team because I was a girl, even though I played better than all of the boys except for Robby Turner. The sports teacher said he was sorry, he knew how much I loved it, "You look like a boy. We could almost get away with it," he said wistfully. That made me feel slightly better. If only he knew that I had sacrificed precious playtimes with my best friend and heartthrob Mandy, to practice with the football team.

Similarly, the head teacher, Mr. Hardcastle took me aside before the end of the fourth year, aged eleven, to tell me that he had wanted to make me Head Girl but couldn't because I played football and that wasn't ladylike so he had chosen Trudy Grantham. She had pretty freckles and red hair tied back in a ponytail. She played jinks and hopscotch and skipping like Mandy. Her nomination came from left field. Who had ever heard of Trudy Grantham? She was shy and never put her hand up in class! And what felt really unfair was that she wasn't even one of us three girls who were chosen to "help" Mr. Hardcastle in the stock cupboard. I was picked to be put over his knee for a spanking. He picked Mandy, of course, to cuddle, and he picked Julie Marshall to count the books. I stuffed down the injustice of it all, gave up football and resigned myself to playing jinks and hopscotch.

For jinks you threw ten metal crosses on the ground, then you had to throw and bounce the red ball in the air. While it was in the air, you had to scoop up a certain number of jinks then catch the ball. Earth shatteringly tedious. I looked longingly over at the boys playing football. Fat Matty Simpson had taken my place. The boys were struggling without me. On the first day that I didn't show up, Mike Thompson, the one who always brought the ball to school, called to me roughly, "Hey Claire, where were you? Matty's taken your spot. He's useless."

There wasn't much I could say, "Well, I can't play on the team, so there doesn't seem much point to practicing."

He paused, "Yeah I suppose it's weird you being a girl 'n everything. Matty's useless. He'll drop dead one of these days. He gets so puffed out. He's good for blocking. That's about it."

The disappointment and understanding in his tone were bittersweet. I missed the camaraderie, the "Goodwin! Shoot! Nice one!" as I belted the ball into the back of the net with the goalie flying in all directions.

Skipping was only slightly less dull than jinx: "One potato, two potato, three potato four," you had to run in and skip for four swings of the rope, then the next girl ran in and you ran out. There were endless rhymes, "I'm a little teapot, short and stout, tip me up and pour me out!"

I barely knew the names of some of these girls. The experience bored me so much. Skipping did however legitimize my being around Mandy and I made sure I never missed a beat with the rope. She inspired me to skip harder, faster, higher…

*Fiona Goodwin*

# CHAPTER THREE

On the morning of the exorcism, I didn't know what to wear. Something comfortable I assumed. I'd seen the film *The Exorcist*, so I had a rough idea of what was going to happen. Loose-fitting clothing would probably be best. The usual combat trousers and oversized smock and lace-up hiking boots seemed inappropriate. Then I remembered that that was all I had. It had rained in the night and the seat of my bicycle was wet. I wiped it with the sleeve of my smock. I unchained the rickety lady's bike from the railings and dropped the chain into the wicker basket in the front of the bike. The flat where I lived off Blackfriar's Lane was above a car wash. Cars were emerging, dripping and shiny. If only there was a human car wash where I could drop money in a slot and come out the other side, pure and clean. I pushed off and swung my leg over the bike. I had lain in bed fretting, unable to sleep most of the night. I was tired. Tired and sad. None of my flat-mates, save Helen, knew about my Saturday assignation. In total, there were seven of us living there, sharing one kitchen, one bathroom, and one electric fire. We all attended the church. We were in our late teens and twenties—two girls, two boys, all students, and three nurses—all nurses were girls in those days. When we weren't studying or working, we held Bible studies and prayer meetings. We pretty much knew everything about each other. The kettle was always on and we took turns cooking up huge batches of spaghetti bolognese and fish pie made of coley, a fish that was usually reserved for cat food. The local fishmonger had adopted us and whispered to me one day, "If you're looking for a cheap fish dinner love, coley's what you want, it's half the price of other fish! Slap some mashed potato on it, you can't beat it!" We were all on a budget and grateful for his advice.

Karen, a jolly paediatric nurse made huge trays of the most amazing chocolate brittle most weekends. On the weekends that she went back to Scotland to visit family, the remainder of us would sit around the kitchen table with mugs of tea and discuss the chocolate brittle, sharing theories about its ingredients, the texture, how it was the best thing we'd ever eaten. We were family and Karen's chocolate brittle was the glue.

A couple of the nurses worked nightshifts, Lydia being one of them. As you know, the kiss happened because we were sharing a single bed to save money. She slept in it during the day and I slept in it at night. On the mornings that I didn't have to be at college early, we overlapped. As our friendship grew, I had found myself lingering in bed, anticipating her warmth. Saturday morning was often one of those days but this Saturday I had to be up early to be up at Pastor Mick's by ten. In any case, he had told me to stay away from her.

It was painful to extract myself from the bed knowing that this day could be the end of my loving her. It put into question my continuing to live and share a bed with her as well as my continuing to live in our little community. I had turned down her invitation that morning to go and see Herman Hesse's film *Siddhartha* at the Curzon in Mayfair.

*Fiona Goodwin*

Saying no to her companionship and our shared love of foreign films was excruciating. I pedaled a few yards then it struck me that cycling home from an exorcism might not be the wisest course of action. It could be similar to when you have an operation. Who knows what state I would be in? What if the demon took me over? I might be bruised or traumatised. I turned back and chained the bike to the railings. I decided to walk to the bus stop.

I picked up the pace at Old Bailey Street, the home of The Old Bailey. This is where all the major criminal trials were held, and still are, since 1584. Such an intimidating building standing on the site of the medieval Newgate Gaol. The stone arches held hundreds of years of foreboding. You had to have done something very grim to be tried here. How terrible to fall foul of the law. It made me wonder about my salvation. I had studied the rapture in the *Book of Revelation* and I had learned about 666, the "mark of the beast." At the second coming of Jesus, those that have accepted to be marked with the 666 will not be taken up in the rapture and God will let the devil rule on earth for a thousand years and then some people will possibly still make it to heaven if they resist Satan during that time, but that will be so difficult that mostly they will succumb and go to hell. I had a book with a map, *The Chronology of the End Times*. It clearly explained in pictures what was going to happen. I knew that those who had not accepted Jesus into their hearts would not be saved. I wrestled with the fate of Muslims and Hindus and atheists who will all go to hell. My friend Ranjit was a Seik, one of the most caring people I knew. I couldn't justify her going to hell but the Bible said that Jesus was the only way. Having said that, my own chances weren't looking that good! It gave me such a headache sometimes, just worrying about it.

In front of the Old Bailey in my heavy wool duffle coat, smock, and combat trousers, I didn't feel confident that I would be able to steer a straight course, no pun intended. Oscar Wilde was tried at the Old Bailey three times for the crime of "sodomy", and after being sentenced to two years hard labour, he moved to France. He never got over it. Something I would never have to endure but eternal damnation wasn't sounding too good, and our church leaders were at pains to let us know that the soul of anyone on that path would be in danger. The original law instituted against homosexuality by Queen Victoria only applied to men. Apparently, she couldn't believe that women would ever be capable of such "abhorrent" behaviour.

Having an exorcism seemed odd to me. It struck me as medieval and I didn't show any of the commonly recognized symptoms of being possessed. I didn't feel that my body was ever involuntarily taken over by an evil spirit. I never frothed at the mouth or screamed obscenities. However, we were taught in the church that Satan disguised himself in many forms and often came to us as a wolf in sheep's clothing. We were told that his cleverest trick was to make the world think that he did not exist, that hell did not exist, that there was no such thing as eternal damnation or consequences for our actions. Not being "unequally yoked" was the most effective way to keep alert to his wiles. This meant that we should have relationships and friendships only with Christians. Non-Christians might weaken our faith or lead us on the wrong path.

We were told the story of how Abraham bowed his head just before following God's instruction to slay his son, Isaac.

*Fiona Goodwin*

The bowing of his head represented the submission of his intellect. We had to let go of our own thinking and accept the word of God and of the church and its leaders. The Bible WAS the inspired word of God. I loved the simplicity of it. I loved having clear instructions to follow and I loved the kindness and authenticity of my Christian friends and teachers. However, my chest would tighten whenever the fear of damnation invaded my thoughts. That felt terrifying. Desolate.

I arrived five minutes early. I was weak with hunger. Mick came down the stairs and his greeting was muted, a perfunctory hug and a sober, "Come on up."

# CHAPTER FOUR

N ow my head was hurting. I felt dizzy going up the stairs. When I saw the suited men gathered in the lounge I was petrified. There was Uncle Ern. No one knew why he was called "Uncle." Standing alongside him was Pastor Mick and Uncle Ern's assistant, Barry. My fear gave way to utter humiliation when, amongst the four men, I recognized the handsome young assistant pastor, Bertie. He was "learning the exorcism ropes." Who asked him to come?! He was the same age as me, this was unbelievably embarrassing! Bertie gave me a formal, "Hello Claire."

I could barely make eye contact. Bertie was the chap I was going to marry if I could get rid of the demon of homosexuality and if he got rid of Liv, his girlfriend. I was directed to an upright wooden chair in the center of the sitting room. Uncle Ern had a loving presence. He was about two inches shorter than me and he reached out his arms and held me close. I clung on, wishing I could disappear. Tears sprung from my eyes and he let go, grabbing the clean white handkerchief from his pocket and reaching up and wiping my eyes. "Come on m' lover, we got work to do today. God loves you and we do, and Jesus is going to deliver you from this thing that's got a hold of you." His lilting Cornish accent was comforting.

I wept again with relief and gratitude. Uncle Ern to the rescue! "You know, don't you m' lover that the Bible says it's a sin to have sexual relations with another woman?"

"Yes," I said.

"And you really 'ave to want to let go of this thing and this perverse way of thinkin'. You do want a nice 'usband one day, don't you Claire? A man who loves God and will be good to you and a good father to your children?"

If only he knew that my potential husband was part of the exorcism team! The dream of having children and a man that would love me, was always there but it never stopped my falling head over heels in love with girls. "Yes, I do want that," I said.

"Wantin' it isn't enough m' lover, you 'ave to choose it every day so the demon don't come back. We could get it out today and you could let it back in tomorrow if you don't truly repent. Is that understood?"

"Yes," I said. I didn't like the sound of that. I thought they would just get it out and I wouldn't have to worry about it ever again. Surely the demon shouldn't be allowed back in after it was cast out?

"So do you believe that where two or three are gathered, God is in the midst? That Jesus is right here? You know Mick and Bertie and this is Derek who's worked with a lot of people who've 'ad this problem. They are all 'ere to pray for you and to get you delivered of this demon. Anything you want to ask before we start m'lover?"

"How do I stop it getting back in?" I asked hesitantly.

"You pray and you keep your eyes on Jesus. This 'omosexuality is a lie of the devil. The truth is that you were made to be with a man. Your body is a holy temple for Jesus that is meant for a man. Pray and be alert. Read the scriptures and if you 'ave any bad thoughts, confess 'em, before it's too late."

"Too late for what?" I thought. Too late to keep the demon out? How many bad thoughts would it take for the demon to get back in? I wanted to know if I would go to hell if the demon came back in but I couldn't keep asking him questions. He had, after all, travelled eight hours the day before on the train from Cornwall and he was doing this to help me. I really should just let them get on with it.

My mind wandered to the fact that Uncle Ern and Aunty Sal had never had children. I had heard on the grapevine that that was their great sorrow and here they were spending their time on people like me. People like me. It was bad enough being such a disappointment to my mother but now I was letting God down, the church, and wasting Uncle Ern's time. Uncle Ern's child would never have caused this trouble. I felt terrible.

"We'll say a prayer before we start." Uncle Ern and Mick stood in front of me, Bertie and Derek behind. I had never had this many men crowd around me. It was both comforting and intimidating. I felt the strength of their intention and their wanting to help.

Uncle Sid started, "Lord I come before thee in the name of our Lord Jesus asking for a miracle 'ere today. We are grateful for the power of prayer and we are grateful that wherever two or three are gathered in your name, there you are in the midst. We bring before you, your daughter Claire, and we ask that the blood of Jesus wash her mind and heart and body clean of this spirit of 'omosexuality. Claire, do you confess your sin and ask Jesus to deliver you in the name of Jesus! Do you truly repent of this wickedness?" I nodded. I couldn't speak. My eyes filled up. I was sorry. Sorry for my sin.

"Right so you'll sit 'ere." He sat me down in the wooden chair in the centre of the room. "We are goin' to pray and we are going to get the demon OUT!"

I jumped out of my skin as he shouted "OUT!" It gave me such a fright. I think he was trying to catch the demon off guard. Then all the men joined in shouting in tongues, "Shalla balla yama sabaloo, onamala, mana shana, dollar ona vasakamala! YES JESUS! Deliver our precious sister in Jeeeeeesus name! In the name of Jeeeeeeeesus!"

There were strong hands on my shoulders pushing down and Uncle Ern's hand on my forehead forcing it back. Maybe that was to open up the airway so the demon could get out more easily? It reminded me of CPR training. I was pouring with tears now, what kind of tears I don't know: despair, repentance, sadness that I was spending my Saturday morning being pushed and shouted at by four grown men instead of being at the cinema with Lydia? Or maybe it was the demon surrendering? God, I hope so! I was desperate for the demon to leave me, I was begging inside. I repeated to myself over and over again, "Let me go! I want to be normal! I don't want this! Jesus, help me!"

Uncle Ern kept pushing my head back but nothing came out. How would I know if it had come out? In the film, Linda Blair vomited green slime. Pauline was so houseproud. I thought about her carpet. It worried me that there was no plastic sheeting. The men's prayers turned to loud commands, "Satan, leave her! Leave our sister Claire! IN THE NAME OF JESUS!"

I could feel the pressure of their hands bearing down on my shoulders and I continued to whimper. The deepest quagmire of grief welling up at all the goodbyes, at all the times I had felt love, felt loved and had had to push it away. My heart was shattered over and over, cratered like the surface of the moon, each indentation, a moment of love that had been aborted. Jesus would show me, wouldn't he? Would he become everything to me so that I could heal and so that my life would no longer be a continual parade of farewells?

The shouting was gaining force, louder as they exhorted the demons to leave me, and never come back. There were new demons and, as each one was named, I felt the truth of it and collapsed into heavy sobs. The spirit of possession! Yes I was possessive! When I loved, I couldn't bear to share. The spirit of Jealousy! I confessed and admitted that I was eaten up with jealousy and now I knew that it was a spirit. Hatred and rebelliousness and God knows what others were invoked and told to leave. I wondered where the demons lived inside of me. I imagined an inky black liquid like the venom of an octopus seeping its way through my mind, my veins, swirling around my beating heart, sinking down to the tips of my toes. I was possessed by evil and it had infiltrated the very core of my being. I seeped tears of despair and impotence. But I had to focus. I had to get the demons out. I must cooperate. I must be willing.

Did loving Lydia make me unwilling? The fear of that tightened around my chest, the fear that I could never stop loving Lydia or Mandy or Debbie or Ellis or... the silent list was endless. Did these men really know what I was feeling? If I told them, would I be expelled from my own exorcism and would that make me a hopeless case? To sin against the Holy Spirit, the New Testament said, was the only unforgivable sin. Was this unforgivable? All this opportunity to be delivered from evil but to be thinking about how much I loved Lydia instead. They said I had to be willing. Was I? Really? I thought about the kiss. It had been my first real kiss. None of the kisses with boys had felt remotely like it. With them I had simply been acting a part, convincing myself and everyone around me that I was normal, while my heart longed to be elsewhere. I longed to be with Lydia. I felt safe with her. I thought of how reassuring it was seeing her in her Sister's uniform with that little watch attached to her white pinafore pocket, her starched tall hat.

At 24, she was in charge of the Intensive Care Unit at St Thomas's Hospital. The night before the kiss, she had invited me to meet her at work at the start of her shift. This is what led to the kiss. A moment of weakness. I had taken the lift up to the fifth floor. There was no way to let her know I was there so I brazenly pushed open the plastic floppy door of the ICU and located her a few beds away tenderly washing the motionless body of a patient. As I surveyed the six bedded ward, I was stopped dead in my tracks. I had entered a place from the future, semi-naked bodies attached by wires to whirring and pumping machines, tubes coming from every orifice, none of them conscious. I teetered slightly as the blood drained from my face and Lydia's strong arm caught me around my waist as I slid down to the shiny floor. She laughed her jolly laugh, "Oh dear Claire! You've turned green!" She supported me to a chair outside and was clearly amused, "I probably should have warned you! You did say you wanted to see where I worked! I'll get you a glass of water." I smiled weakly. I felt the strength of her arm around me. I wanted to cry.

I lay in bed that night, unable to sleep, I was anticipating her return more than I usually did. I wanted to feel her physically close again. I was scared of what that might mean…

My reverie was broken by a crescendo of shouting and pushing as the four praying men bellowed at the demon of anger. Anger! Oh yes, and that's when I flashed, "You want anger? Here it is! Bugger off, you bastards! You bloody bastards!" I screamed. I never swore normally. It must have been the devil taking over! But I wasn't screaming at demons, I was screaming at the men holding me down. This was the moment that I thought maybe finally something was happening. Rage came all the way up from my lace-up boots and out in a volley of expletives. Finally, my exorcism was starting to look like the movie. This was hopeful. I would look and sound, like a demon-possessed person. The men were trying so hard and I wanted to encourage them. They fired at me: "The blood of Jesus is against you Satan! Come out now! COME OUT! COME OUT!"

Come out? The irony wasn't lost on me. I fired back at them, "Get your bloody hands off me, you bastards!" I wanted it over with. I had a flash of inspiration. I thought I should just let it all out. I mustered all my strength and, pulling out from under their grip on my shoulders, I lunged forward and wrapped my hands around Uncle Ern's scrawny neck. I squeezed hard, strangling him. I had never felt such rage. It was exhilarating and frightening and I was convinced that the demon was showing itself.

The four men grabbed my arms and pulled me back on the seat as their shouting got louder and they were addressing each of the demons by name. The strength of their grip triggered terror. I was being physically restrained. I didn't recognize myself. I calmed myself by thinking about my evening plan to watch Moonlighting that night, the American TV series with Cybill Shepherd and Bruce Willis. Thinking of Cybil made me think of Sybil the woman with multiple personality disorders. My deliverers seemed encouraged by my violence. They clearly felt that the forces of darkness were finally making themselves known. My throat was sore.

They too were sounding more and more hoarse, "We defy you Satan, you have no power over this child of God, she does not belong to you! Let her go! Come out! Come out!"

The shouting started to die down and then through their legs, I saw Pauline. I knew it was Pauline because of her leg. What was depressing about this was that we had prayed for Pauline's leg, week in and week out in the church, and Pauline's leg was just getting bigger. And I thought, shouldn't we be praying for Pauline's leg instead of praying for me to stop loving Lydia?

"Cup of tea anyone?" she asked.

I really wasn't sure where we were in the proceedings but we all definitely needed some liquid refreshment.

I lifted up my tear-stained face to see Uncle Ern nod to her, "Good idea m'lover."

There was no eye contact as the men lowered themselves into the sofa behind me at the back of the room. I remained alone in the middle of the room on the wooden chair. They seemed depleted. The teapot and cups were Royal Worcester with a pink rose motif and gold trim. Pauline swilled the pot around a little to strengthen the tea and rested the silver tea strainer as she poured into each cup. The ritual was soothing.

There were no demons in the teapot. I wondered if her leg hurt or if a demon did that to her or was it because she had sinned. I felt relief that I didn't have something apparently incurable like Pauline. At least Uncle Ern said I could be cured.

Pauline lifted up a plate, "Biscuits anyone? I've got pink wafers, rich tea, custard creams, crunch creams, ginger creams, Breakaways—them's the ones in the yellow wrapper, the Viennese Whirls, they're m' favourite."

I wanted to eat the whole plate but I just took a couple. I dunked the rich tea and expertly popped it in my mouth before it collapsed. I didn't dunk the Custard cream—they don't need it because of the cream filling. I wolfed down one of each and went back for a Breakaway.

"Another one?" Pauline was waving the teapot.

"Yes, another drop would be lovely," said Derek.

I held out my cup and saucer and Pauline poured in the tea through the strainer then brought me the china jug of milk.

"Sorry to put the tea in first, lovey," I smiled a 'don't worry' at her.

What would happen now? I was feeling a bit sick from all the biscuits and the crying and shouting.

Nothing was said. We silently sipped and replaced our cups on the coffee table in the centre of the room. As I got up, I felt the soreness in my arms and I wondered if I had bruises.

"All right m' lover, we'll have a bit more of a go and then we'll call it a day."

A bit more of a go? I was awash with tea and biscuits. They gathered around again and more gently this time, beseeched the Holy Ghost and Jesus and the Lord God Almighty to "have mercy on a sinner." The prayers were now kinder, quieter. No hands on me, their arms were in the air. Out of my peripheral vision, I saw faces raised to the ceiling, then, after five minutes or so, Uncle Ern slowly lowered himself into the armchair. "Take a seat everyone."

The men retreated to their sofa behind me. I felt uncomfortable. I quietly rasped, "How did it go, Uncle Ern?" I was hopeful. He breathed deeply, "Not well m' lover."

"Not well? What do you mean, not well?"

"Well m' lover, when we started you had seven demons."

"Wow! And?" I still had hope.

"While we were praying m'lover…five more came in."

I froze. My insides turned to jelly. A cloud of liquid ink descended over me. This could not be true, this was not happening. I steeled myself. These soothing words ran through my head, "I can stop caring. I can leave. I don't have to listen to these men anymore." But would God be merciful, I wondered?

"Sorry, m' lover. You 'ave to be really willing to let the demon go."

Willing? Was it my fault? I wasn't willing?! I suddenly felt tired and hungry and sick from the biscuits. I needed to get away. I headed for the door and Pauline handed me my coat and I let myself out. As I was walking to the bus stop, I heard Dante's words at the gates of hell, "Abandon hope, all ye who enter here." I thought to myself, "I'm going to be completely alone now, I can never love again. I will never have children, I will never have a family. The devil has a hold of me and I am forever damned."

As the bus approached, I didn't know whether to get on it… or to walk in front of it.

I got off at Marble arch, and there were the Golden Arches. I loved McDonald's. It felt familiar, dependable, nobody there knew there was anything wrong with me and besides I loved burgers. There was the bun, the meat, the cheese, some kind of vegetable and I did something unusual that day of the exorcism, I got the meal deal: a quarter pounder with cheese, medium fries, and a diet coke. In those days the pies were marked "DANGER THIS PIE IS HOT!" Nothing mattered anymore. What the hell did I have to lose? I threw caution to the wind. I ordered a cherry pie…

# CHAPTER FIVE

The convent was in the Italian alps, nestled at the top of a mountain overlooking Lago Maggiore. It was white stone, simple, unornate. There was a one hundred and eighty degree view of the lake and valley. Each morning at 4 a.m. I rolled out of the metal sprung bed, threw on the black skirt and white blouse (the uniform of the novitiate) and made my way to chapel. I crunched across the loose gravel courtyard breathing in the sacredness of the rising sun and mountain air. The sky was a mass of oranges and reds and growing light. I felt safe. I was on my path. I was training for holy orders. The failed exorcism had given me no choice. Maybe here I would find the willingness to let go of the demon. Being celibate and cloistering myself was the only path open to me. I was safe in the arms of God. Never again would I spiritually, or emotionally, harm myself or those I loved by leading them into a relationship that the Bible forbade. I thought of my evangelist idol, Kathryn Kulhman. She could fill entire football stadiums with Christians, she would point at them and they would all fall down. Like her, I would empty myself of my wrong desires and dedicate myself to God's ministry.

I embraced the solitude and the routine of prayer four times a day. The relief of knowing that I was no longer a liability lifted my spirits. I kept away from the other nuns. They were all much older than me, kindly mother figures and thankfully physically unattractive to me. Every Saturday, the old rickety bus would make its way up the windy mountain road full of pilgrims seeking consolation and healing. One morning, a woman came running into the chapel. She was pushing an empty wheelchair, laughing and crying and pointing at her legs. "Suora Chiara! Vedi cos'a fatto il Signore!" Sister Claire! Look what the Lord has done! I can walk! Grazie al Signore!

I had no idea how it had happened, just that I had prayed for her the night before! Maybe I was going to be a healer after all! I was ecstatic and so was the Mother Superior. She invited me to her quarters. We ate hot dogs and watched "Now Voyager" on her little black and white television. Mother Elena's obsession with black and white Hollywood movies was the icing on the cake as far as I was concerned. A life of service and prayer and Bette Davis movies—bliss!

I fell in love at the convent, not just with Bette Davis, I fell in love with the mountains, the relief from inner torment, and the thirty-foot statue of the Virgin Mary. I spent hours at her feet weeping and pleading for transformation and guidance. She became my confessor. She watched over the valley and the scattered villages below, and now me.

I am remembering now that oasis of peace and deep connection at twenty-one, the stark white-washed walls of my cell, the iron frame bed, the scruffy bedside table and drawers and the two-foot oak cross on the wall, and an equally stark wooden chair over which I draped my clothes before sleep. My life mapped out, I felt no need of anything that the world had to offer—prayer and my room, built into the rock was the only sanctuary that I required.

One morning, kneeling before the statue, I got an uneasy feeling. My Bible fell open at 2 Kings 22 verse 2, "David walked in all the way of his father Saul, neither turning to the left nor the right." A cold chill went right through me. It nagged at me for months. Devastated, it eventually dawned on me that being at the convent was "turning to the left or the right." I felt deep inside that I was being called to live my life in the "real world." How was that even possible? I saw no other life for me outside the convent. I had come here because there was no future for me in "normal" society.

One fateful morning before the 4 a.m. call to prayer, I slipped into my sweater and blue jeans. I draped the black skirt and white blouse over the back of the chair. While it was still dark, I went and knelt at the foot of the statue of Mary. I confessed, "You know, I thought I had it all worked out. I wanted to stay here with you, safe from myself. But I have to go." I silently sobbed. I said I was sorry. Sorry for who I was, sorry that I had to go, sorry that I was so powerless over my own nature. I asked her to give me strength. I hoped she would remember me, pray for me. I crept out. I waved down a passing farm vehicle and headed straight down the mountain to the railway station. Back in London, a few days later, heartbroken, I wandered down Oxford Street, praying for a sign, it didn't take long for me to find it—it was an actual neon sign!

"LEARN TOUCH TYPING IN TEN DAYS"

I signed up on the spot. Typing turned into teacher training. Children became my new parish. I loved them, especially the misfits. I held on to Bette Davis' words, "Don't let's ask for the moon. We have the stars…"

# CHAPTER SIX

I hadn't been teaching long when I put a payment down on a house outside of London. On a teacher's salary and a borrowed thousand pounds deposit you could do that in those days. I was soon the worship leader of a local house church, I had my own car and was regularly woken in the night by the drug addicts from the church who recognized my need to be needed. I often spoke at the church, prophesied and gave out words of knowledge—that's the Christian version of being psychic, it's Christian fortune-telling. The non-Christian version is demonic of course. There were about fifteen in the church but it soon grew.

At my first teaching post, Jim was the Physical Education teacher, rippling with muscles. He was also northern. Not being physically attracted to him, I felt comfortable squeezing his biceps on our second meeting. With a sharp intake of breath, I gushed, "What *have* you been doing Jim? You must *live* at the gym!" I flexed my right arm for him, "you should feel my muscles!"

"Not bad Miss G!" he said laughing.

I think I was flirting. No, I know I was flirting. I had to. I was creating a cover. I was combatting the growing infatuation that I felt for Louisa, the girl I had met at the cycling club. It was impossible to stop thinking about her. She was funny and stunningly beautiful.

My very first meeting with Jim was in the corridor outside our classrooms. A belligerent thirteen-year-old boy was refusing to move out of the corridor to go outside for morning break. I was red in the face with fury. The boy was sneering at me. He was vile. I yelled, "Get out NOW!"

Jim, hearing the commotion, came out of his classroom, walked up to the boy and put his arm around his shoulder, "Now, Kenny, you know better than this, Miss Goodwin is new here and we don't want her to get the wrong impression about you, do we? You better apologise to her and then do as you're told, ok?" His voice was warm and calm.

Kenny's head dropped in shame, "Sorry Sir."

"No Kenny, you're apologizing to Miss Goodwin, not me."

"Sorry Miss" His eyes were averted.

"It's Miss *Goodwin* to you Kenny, and look at her while you're saying it." Kenny looked up. "Sorry Miss Goodwin, I'll go out now." It wasn't the same boy that I had screamed at. He turned and left. And I was left wondering how Jim had performed this magic trick.

He introduced himself, "I'm Jim, and that was Kenny. Kenny's mum walked out on him and his Dad, a few weeks ago. He's not doing great. Sorry you got the wrong end of that."

Now I felt bad, embarrassed at how out of control I had been. "Well thanks, I'm Fiona." I was still churned up. I would have liked Jim to put his arm around me.

He seemed to sense my discomfort, "Let's get you a cup of tea." We walked to the staffroom with him chivvying kids to leave the building, "Come on lads, out you go."

"Yes Sir." They looked at him and then looked at me and raised their eyebrows with approval, "YESSS SIR!" We were considered to be an item from day one and that suited me. Jim started driving me to school. We would arrive together and the kids waved and cheered as we drove in the school gate.

I had it all under control I thought. On Sundays, I went to watch him play rugby. I stood on the sidelines holding his sweater, cheering, like a girlfriend, but I wasn't. He was kinder than I was and I studied his kindness, intrigued. He was kind to everyone, the dinner ladies, Mr. Jones the mean caretaker, and of course Kenny, and there were lots more "Kenny's." He would spend his lunchtimes either coaching football or sitting with the strays, the troublemakers. One morning he announced, "I'm taking the bottom set to the Lake District on a geography field trip in a few weeks. I need a female teacher, do you want to come?"

"Is Kenny going?" I asked.

"Yes, Kenny's going," he nodded a smile. "Is that a problem?"

"Not at all. Count me in." I wanted to be with this man and his kindness. I wanted to see him in action with these children.

"Wow, I wasn't expecting that!" he said.

"I love the Lake District." It wasn't a lie but it wasn't the truth either. It dawned on me that, like these children, I just wanted to be in his orbit.

"Ok then, tomorrow we have to get you some walking boots and they will have to be broken in. We'll walk the towpath by the river on Sunday after church." He went to the Catholic Church and I was the worship leader at the charismatic house fellowship. My friends weren't sure that Jim was a real Christian because he wasn't born again and because Catholics were deceived by Satan. They were idolaters, worshipping the Virgin Mary instead of Jesus.

He would possibly go to hell if he didn't ask Jesus into his heart. That was hard to reconcile so I tried to push it out of my mind.

A week before the trip, Jim came to the house, "We need to get you packed. I want to make sure you have the right stuff." We went up to my bedroom. I sat on the edge of the bed while he went through my drawers, "You'll need five pairs of underpants," he was counting as he pulled them out of my underwear drawer. "Are these the warmest you've got?"

"Yes," I replied.

"Then you'll have to double up. What about socks? You need a thin pair to go under the hiking socks that we bought." Having picked out the clothes for the four days, he was satisfied I had everything I needed. "I'll give you one of my sweatshirts and a waterproof. Yours won't last five minutes."

I had a huge urge to put my arms around him, but I just sat there. I wanted him to hold me. I felt a lump in my throat. He stood up, "I'm starving, have you got anything to eat?" I was relieved at the opportunity to break the moment.

I pushed myself up off the bed and headed for the stairs, "Baked beans?!"

"That'll do it!"

"Baked beans on toast, coming up Sir!" I was impersonating Kenny. He laughed and followed me down the stairs.

In the kitchen, Jim opened a drawer and found the tin opener, "You make the toast, I'll do the beans. This is good practice for the field trip!" We ate and then I drank tea while he washed up the dishes. He let himself out with a wave and a cheery, "See you in the morning Miss G! Thanks for dinner!"

He never made a move, I didn't know if he was attracted to me or not. I wondered, as my affection grew, if I was attracted to him. We were so different. I was aloof and uptight and he was friendly and northern. And then, of course, there was Louisa at the cycling club. If only I felt about Jim, the way I felt about her. Maybe that would come…

# CHAPTER SEVEN

The field trip was as much fun as I had ever had. I was his student, watching him as the wayward boys and girls became putty in his hands. On our return, the other kids complained,

"We want a trip, Sir. You only like the naughty kids, Sir! It's not fair!"

So that summer, we booked a PGL adventure holiday in the south of France. Jim and I, in our mid-twenties, were the parents of forty-two teenagers for ten days, canoeing, sailing, and horse-riding. A couple of older, more experienced teachers came to supervise, *us* as much as the kids, I think. There was no time for us to socialise. We were run off our feet and up most of the night, patrolling the boys and girls as they tried to sneak into each other's tents.

On the Saturday night, I said to Jim, "It's Sunday tomorrow, why don't we have church here? Most of these kids have never been to church. We could invite them?"

He was all for it, "Ok, well you will have to do the talking, you know I'm not the preacher-type."

Jim announced at dinner, "Miss G and I are doing a church service on the beach at 8 am tomorrow if anyone wants to come."

They looked bewildered. Marcus, the good-looking football star seemed to be speaking for all of them, "Church?

Really Sir? Anyway, it's too early, Sir!"

Kenny, who was sat at Jim's feet called out, "Is it a wedding, Sir?!" All the kids fell about laughing, looking for my reaction.

"No Kenny," Jim came back quickly, "not unless you're marrying Julie!"

The kids laughed even more, "Sir got you good, Kenny!" Kenny blushed, "Aww! Shut up, sir!" Jim tussled Kenny's hair, "Sorry mate, you asked for that!"

Denise, the friendless, library monitor sidled up to us after dinner, "Sir, Miss, I'm coming to the church thing in the morning. I've never been to church."

"That's lovely, Denise," Jim replied, "we look forward to having you there."

Denise blushed, and then awkwardly wandered off, "Thank you, Sir."

Sunday, Jim and I were out early on the beach. We set up two chairs for ourselves, a ghetto blaster, and Jim had a Bible. We had planned to have it early, deliberately, so only the kids who were truly interested would come.

From where we were sitting we could see the tents. No one was stirring.

"Looks like it's just me, you and Jesus…or should I say the Virgin Mary." I grinned cheekily.

"Watch it, young lady!" Jim launched himself and threw me down in the sand. "Don't you be taking Our Lady's name in vain!" That's when we heard Kenny, "Oy! Sir! What you doing to Miss?! Thought you said it was church! Funny kind of church if you ask me!" He was beaming from ear to ear, bleary-eyed, still in pyjamas, dragging his sleeping bag across the sand. Following some way behind was Denise, in her floral nightie. They installed themselves on the sand, in what they deemed to be the front row. Kenny's voice must have done the job of the church bells because a trickle of other kids started, all in various states of sleepiness, till finally, all forty-two children were sat, some laying on sleeping bags, in front of us, looking up expectantly, waiting for "church." I don't know why it was so moving, but it was. I felt so much love for these children. They sat in complete silence listening to the CD of John Lennon singing, "Imagine all the people, living in this world..." and as the song ended, Jim started reading, "If I have faith that can move mountains, but do not have love, I am nothing. If I give all I possess to the poor and give over my body to hardship, but do not have love, I am nothing." He continued, "Love is patient, love is kind..." all the way to the end of 1 Corinthians 13.

I was watching the sixteen-year-old football stars as they gazed at their hero, taking it in. You could have heard a pin drop. I had never met anyone who embodied those words as fully as Jim did. I never heard him lose his temper or say a sharp word to anyone.

It was my turn to speak. I felt inspired and strangely humbled, "Mr. Jones just read the most important words that we may ever hear. Some of you are rich and clever and good at football and whilst those are great things, none of that really matters if we don't have love. Some of us may be poor and not so good at football..."

A hand went up, it was Kenny, "That would be me, Miss!" Everyone laughed. "And me," came from a few others...

I continued, "But if we have love we are richer than anyone. I am now going to pray and you may want to close your eyes." I prayed, "Dear God, whoever you are, thank you for everyone here, for this beach, for the sun and the sand and the sea, thank you for the love that we have for each other and for being here with us now. We are asking you to help us to be more loving. We ask that that love will be the guiding force in our lives. Please bless all these children, and the people that care for them, bless Mr. Jones, and myself." I continued, "We are going to have a couple of minutes of silence and if you want to you can pray your own prayer."

There was now just the sound of the waves and the sea breeze. Kenny was looking around to see what everyone else was doing. Their heads were bowed, so he lowered his.

And then something magical happened. From the other end of the beach, we heard the sound of a radio and Phil Collins singing, "I can feel it coming in the air tonight. Oh Lord, And I've been waiting for this moment all my life, Oh Lord…" It was spooky. Wide-eyed, the kids looked up, even the handsome football stars. I felt chills go through me. It felt as if we had been visited. It was a confirmation to me that I was finally on the right path and that Jim was on that path with me. I had to make this work.

# CHAPTER EIGHT

The problem was Louisa. She was the fly in the ointment of my perfect plan. On some Saturday mornings when Jim went to play rugby, I went cycling, and so did Louisa. She had a flashy, blue Rock Hopper mountain bike. I was powerless over the way I felt about her. My heart burst with happiness when I saw her. She was Italian. Being around her was exhilarating. She had that accent, and black hair, and those dark eyes.

"You no bring your boyfriend to cycle club, why?" It was an innocent question but she had a cheeky grin, which disarmed me.

I stuttered. "He plays rugby." Jim at this point wasn't exactly my boyfriend but I wanted her to think he was.

"Ah, he play rugby... and that is the reason you no bring him?" She looked disbelieving.

What was she getting at?" She was a couple of years older than me. She was pedaling fast. Keeping up with her was tough. We had crept to the front of the pack.

"Claire, you try keep up!" She turned to look at me and winked. I was flustered. It felt like flirting, my stomach was doing somersaults, and that lasted for all of the twenty-five miles of country lanes.

"You want to get beer at pub? Or you got to get back to boyfriend?" She was talking as if she didn't believe I had a boyfriend.

"No, I don't have to get back to *boyfriend!*" I imitated her accent.

"Great, I buy you beer and beautiful Breetish pork pie! You like?" She could have offered me a handful of stinging nettles and I would have eaten them.

"Sure thanks." I feigned just the right amount of indifference.

We sat outside the seventeenth century pub at a pitted oak trestle table. I was relieved to see the other cyclists head for a different table. Dear God. This is all wrong. I shouldn't feel *this* happy!

She emerged from the pub with the beers and pork pie, "We share pork pie, too big for one person." My heart was beating out of my chest. That familiar feeling…

"I don't know why I love pork pie!" she raved. "It's made of *sheet! Sheet* on the outside and pig *sheet* on the inside but my God, it taste good!" We laughed. She broke the pork pie in half, "Open your mouth." I went along with her feeding me and bit into the pie, she took a sharp intake of breath, "My God you have such beautiful blue eyes! Did you know that Claire? Did anyone ever tell you that before?"

"Umm, I don't think so." I hid my blushing and took a swig of beer. I had lied again. My eyes had been mentioned but never had it made me feel dizzy! We chatted. She sat close as she told me about her research work at the university. When there was no beer or porkpie left, we lingered.

"Where you live?" she asked. I told her. I wanted to invite her home but Jim was coming over and in any case, how could I, when she made me feel the way she did?

She saw me, deliberating, "I know, you got boyfriend. Maybe I come another day…"

*Fiona Goodwin*

"That would be lovely." I reverted to being polite. I had to get away before I said something stupid or changed my mind. I was doing well with Jim. I didn't want to mess it up.

I took Jim's interest and devotion for granted for as long as I could until an evening walk in the local park where he told me that he was applying for another job. I panicked. I asked him why, and he said, "I have nothing to keep me here."

It was a balmy summer evening and we stood on Putney Bridge overlooking the Thames. I looked at the green, murky water and thought of a life without his warmth. I felt stung by the abandonment. I wept, something I never did. I didn't want him to go and I hadn't known till then how much he meant to me. He put his arms around me. I felt safe and the water below twinkled with the reflection of the street lamps.

I told him, "I don't want you to go." I turned my face towards him and our eyes locked. After what seemed ages, we kissed. That was all the persuading he needed to keep him from leaving. I was grateful and from then on to all intents and purposes, we were boyfriend and girlfriend.

Jim was the most loving man I have ever known. He showed me how unloving and critical I was without ever saying an unkind word to me. Even when I started to open up to him and suggest that maybe I was a little shut down, he acted as if he had no idea what I was talking about. I would spend evenings at his flat and we would end up in bed and I enjoyed making out with him, but with his being a catholic, there was no penetration. That suited me. If we got aroused or one of us had an orgasm, he would confess to the priest the next day. That would make it all right. I had no feeling that we would be together forever for so many reasons. He was a catholic and my brand of Christianity said that Catholics were in the clutches of Satan because they worshipped Mary. Many of my Christian friends questioned his salvation. They were concerned that he would go to hell. They reminded me that I could not be "unevenly yoked" and that his 'worshipping Mary' could damage my walk with Jesus. In some ways, I thought that what we did in bed, which wasn't much, was less likely to get me damned than my thoughts about Louisa. I decided to solidify my effort to be heterosexual by introducing Jim to my Mother. If he survived her scrutiny we would be home free! Taking him to see her was the next step on the path to being normal.

# CHAPTER NINE

Mother was waiting expectantly on the porch as we arrived. The floral pattern on her dress matched the pink roses trained over the doorway. She was fiddling with a gold necklace over her plunging neckline. I had warned Jim in advance, "See what I mean about her cleavage?!" I giggled.

"Ay, she's got a lot to be proud of," Jim whispered back. We got out of the car and crunched down the long gravel drive to meet her.

"Hello darling," she kissed me firmly on the cheek and then, "and you must be Jim?"

"Ay, lovely to meet you."

She giggled like a schoolgirl, then flinched slightly, hearing his northern accent. She shook his hand.

"Oh God it's started," I thought.

Off she went with her Red Riding Hood wolf greeting, "What lovely curly hair you have, Jim!" that warm yet sinister tone that was reserved for new partners. They think she's being lovely, but she's playing with them, lulling them into a false sense of security, before swallowing them alive.

We were led to the lounge where the teacups were already in place on the tray, a posy of pink roses in a small vase. The sofa pattern matched the pink flowers. They were everywhere. The scene was set.

"Cup of tea, Jim?"

"Lovely, Faith."

Oh God, I panicked, he's calling her Faith. He should have called her Mrs. Finch.

"Do you take sugar, Jim?"

"No thanks"

"Sweet enough, is that it Jim?" She smiled that exocet missile smile.

He laughed kindly, "That's right, Faith."

Oh God! It would be better not to call her anything than call her Faith. We all sank into the deep flowery armchairs and sofa.

David, my handsome stepfather, loomed in the doorway of the lounge, and we all struggled to get up again. He said, too late, "Don't get up. Hello Jim, I hear you're a colleague of Claire's. Nice of you to bring her over. She usually has too much marking to do, don't you, Claire?" There was the first dig. He said it not for himself, he said it for mother. She was his raison d'être.

Mother continued her assault, "Jim spends a lot of time in the gym, don't you Jim! What a perfect name!" She laughed at her own joke, "He's a PE teacher David, so he doesn't have to do any reading or writing, is that right Jim?"

She was really going for it. Her tone was sweet but the undercurrent demeaning. I wanted to defend him with, "But he also teaches geography!" I knew it was pointless and would sound desperate.

Tea and homemade lemon drizzle cake were followed by mother's invitation to watch the television, "There's a lovely educational Horizon programme on at five that David and I have been watching. I think we might all enjoy it. It's about earthquakes and the plate system. Would you like to see it, Jim?"

It was a rhetorical question. I held my breath and then sighed inwardly as he responded, "That sounds interesting, Faith."

Oh God, I wish he would stop calling her Faith!

The folding doors of the television were swung open, evidence of their not being big television watchers. Buttons were pressed and there was a reverential silence as the Horizon opening credits rolled. All was going well until five minutes into the programme, Jim picked up the newspaper from the coffee table and started reading the back page, the sports page no less! I felt paralysed with fear. What the hell was he doing?! Mother was fidgety and on him like a hawk, "Jim, are you not enjoying the programme?"

Barely looking up from the paper, he said, "No, it's great Faith, I just realized I hadn't checked the scores today. Oh God, he was talking about football!

My heart was pounding. What would she do now? Why couldn't he just watch the programme instead of being difficult?

"Ah," she continued, feigning comprehension, and with a hint of a sneer, "and do you do the football pools, Jim?" It was a direct insult. Looking up from the paper, he gave her a wide smile, "No Faith, do you?"

She flinched again but quickly regrouped, "No actually I don't," and rallied with, "Jim, did you go to university?" Her tone was cool.

"I did, Faith. I went to Leeds."

She winced (Leeds is in the north.) John looked back down at the paper and added almost as an afterthought, "And then Harvard." She almost spat out her tea, eyes wide with joy, "Harvard? Really?!" She beamed across at David, then raced on, "And what were you studying?"

"I wasn't studying, Faith," there was a dramatic pause, "I was teaching."

"Teaching?! At Harvard?!" Her face was now bright pink. She clutched at her necklace, running it from side to side through her fingers. He was no longer the village idiot. She was almost breathless, "What were you teaching John and how long were you there?"

John looked up again, held her gaze, and solemnly said, "I was teaching football, Faith, it was a two week holiday camp for kids."

Her whole body slumped. She let go of the necklace. He had out-maneuvered her. He wasn't intimidated, and I loved him for that. He had passed the test, mine at least.

After dinner, Mother wanted to show off the river at the bottom of the garden, "Claire, go and show Jim the garden." I lurched to my feet, grateful for the escape, but honestly, that was always my kneejerk response to any request she made. Jim was starting to tire of the stage-managing and he too, was looking for an "out," so he willingly followed her lead.

She opened the back door, "Off you go, you two! I'll have a nice pot of Earl Grey and a Victoria sponge ready for you when you get back."

Tea and cake were how she showed her love, but I wanted to punch her. I often wanted to punch her. I remember the rage being there as far back as twelve. My remedy then was ingenious. I would run out of the house at night and crash into the darkness of the woods. It was so black that I would blindly force my way through the dense foliage, deeper and deeper into the forest, risking scratches and spiders in my hair. The anger propelled me. I was King Kong divesting myself of a murderous fury. I used the terror of the dark to neutralise the anger, which would eventually subside. I thought at times that my heart would implode with the pressure, but terror became my friend and forced me back to the house. I would sprint, utterly panicked, convinced that I was being chased by a killer in those ominous shadows. Back at the well-lit doorway, I was just grateful to be safe and to feel calm again.

Down in the garden with Jim, and out of earshot, I started, "Oh my God, she sends me round the twist!"

He took my hand, "Claire, she's just an uptight southerner. A harmless nutter." He grinned cheekily.

"You have no idea," I said.

# CHAPTER TEN

I should have mentioned that I was called Fiona till I was eight and then Claire till I was thirty-three. It was on my eighth birthday, Christopher (my older brother) and I, were sat to attention at the dining room table. He was ten, my mother thirty-two. She called through the hatch, "Are you ready?!"

We had devoured her delicious still warm sausage rolls and strawberry jelly and cream and now it was time for cake! We shouted back, "Ready!"

Mother sang with gusto as she emerged from the kitchen, candles fluttering, "Happy birthday to you! Happy birthday to you! Happy birthday dear Fiona, Happy birthday to you!"

She made the best chocolate cake, with just the right amount of icing. She knew it was my favourite. I loved how she could make an occasion, any occasion, feel special and grand! She was radiant in the glow of the candles, eyes wide, beaming from ear to ear. She was such a beautiful woman. She came out in a cream, sheer blouse, leading always with her cleavage—this day was no exception. There was nothing quite like bathing in the focus of her joy and adoration. From experience, we were careful not to spoil those moments by being anything less than utterly appreciative. We never knew how long they would last.

She placed the cake triumphantly onto the cloth lace doily, "Look!" she cried.

We looked. We knew to gasp with awe. As always, there would be a loving message inscribed in white icing against the dark of the chocolate. Our eyes went to the message, it said, "HAPPY BIRTHDAY *CLAIRE!*"

Nobody spoke. Christopher and I knew not to look at each other. We had no idea how to react. Claire was my middle name. Till now, no one had ever called me Claire.

"That's lovely Mummy!" I used my most grateful voice, but I was bewildered.

Christopher, without missing a beat, echoed, "Yes that's lovely Mummy!" and he smoothly followed it up with, "And that's nice to put *Claire.*

Mother tilted her head and gushed, "Darling, I thought it would be lovely to change your name to Claire now. What do you think?"

I knew this was not a choice, the name was clearly written in icing on the cake.

"Yes, that sounds lovely, Mummy."

Disagreeing or throwing cold water on an idea that was thrilling to her would ruin the moment, or to be more accurate, would ruin her moment. Mother's moods could last for days. Holding on to my name wasn't worth that. "Shall I cut it now, Mummy?" I was anxious to remain enthusiastic.

"Good idea, darling!" She was so happy with her plan.

"About time!" Christopher chimed in.

Within a week all our relatives and friends were informed of the name change. Nothing more was said about it for twenty-five years. To seal the deal, a few days later my long blond hair was cut off. I'm not aware of having any opinion about any of this at the time except that I wanted more than anything to make Mother happy—and my being reinvented as Claire, clearly did that. NOT making her happy was a terrifying and miserable prospect; the cloud that would enshroud me at those times lasted for weeks and plunged me into a dark vortex of loneliness. Christopher and I would snatch a few words at the top of the stairs before we went into our separate bedrooms but those moments aside, there was little companionship. When I tracked down my father in my early twenties, I stayed at his house. He was nothing like Mother had described him. I found myself uncontrollably sobbing in the night so I tentatively tapped on his door to wake him. I meant to ask him why he had left us, but instead, I sobbed, "Why did you leave us with *her*?!"

I think the name change was the nail in the coffin of any sense of self, along with the drastic chopping off of my long hair. It felt like the beginning of a willingness to abdicate my own desires. It was the only path to peace and as a result, I became proficient at identifying the needs of others whilst shelving my own. I learned to be charming and detached and to play dead. I learned to love and leave easily, in many cases too easily. It meant that when the Christians found me when I was fifteen, I had a void waiting to be filled. I was searching for meaning, searching for God. I knew that human love was fickle and not to be trusted. My motto was: "Every silver lining has a cloud." It made it easy to go to the convent, abstinence came naturally and, let's face it, a relationship with a girl was not a path that was open to me so I had little to lose. Schooling myself out of sexual desire was not a big stretch. Being straight seemed doable. Mostly, I discovered young the power of reinvention. I have Mother to thank for that.

Christopher at least had an opinion about my hair, "You look like Illya Kuryakin from The Man from Uncle." Mother giggled.

I don't think he meant it as a compliment, but I was delighted. David McCullum, the actor, was my role model. The toy replica of his gun was my best Christmas gift ever.

# CHAPTER ELEVEN

Jim and I were gazing into the river. I let the memory of the cake and the changing of my name flow out of my mind and into the gentle current. I was no longer a child, I was a twenty-three-year-old woman, standing next to a good man, a great man, to whom I wasn't attracted. Having my hand in his was at once soothing and disturbing. I knew mother was watching. She would see now that I was loved by a man, I was normal. However, her jealousy could be aroused and that would have consequences. I felt her eyes boring into the back of me. Gazing into the slow-moving river, Jim put his arm around me. He felt me stiffen, and let go. "You're a funny old girl, what are you so scared of?"

There was no edge to his voice, ever. He looked into my eyes. I looked down. My eyes filled up. He put his hand on my shoulder like he would with Kenny or Denise. I couldn't speak. He never said stupid things like," You know you can trust me," or, "you know you can talk to me." He just waited. And when I didn't speak, he gently squeezed my shoulder, "Shall we go and have that cup of tea?"

I wiped my eyes and nodded. He took my hand and walked me back to the house. I loved that he didn't take my frigidity personally.

That night he encouraged me to go back to his flat to sleep and I lay in his arms and cried like a baby. He had

*Fiona Goodwin*

stopped asking why and just held me. I eventually heard his breath change as he fell into a deep sleep. I felt abandoned as his arms became limp and loosened around me. I missed him when he slept.

At that time, I was regularly overcome with tears and grief. My sarcastic, cynical exterior was melting, defenseless against his steadfastness. Often, in those days I had no idea why I was crying, just that with him, it was safe to do so.

I had never known such constancy. No moods. Not from him at least. It would be hard to find a better man. I had his admiration and felt a deep sense of security. The absence of any real chemistry I tried to put out of my mind. I attributed the lack of passion on my side to my childhood, to the absence of my father growing up, to my stepfather who felt distant, and to this quicksand of a mother. It was no wonder I could be aloof and cold. And then there were the demons. The demons! Some nights I lay wondering where they were. I knew they were lurking, waiting to get me. I knew that because of Louisa, because of how I felt about her.

The following week, I told Jim that the bike ride would be a much longer one and that I wouldn't be home till later. I lied. I lied to that good man who didn't have a dishonest bone in his body. I now had no moral compass apparently. I felt happy and appalled at myself all at once. Louisa came back to the house. We sat on my postage stamp lawn and drank tea and ate scones and cream. Her dark eyes flashed in the sun, she was intoxicating. As I reached to take her empty plate, she took my hand. I didn't fight her, I just worried that the garden wall was not high enough, that the neighbours might see. She cradled my hand in hers until a ladybird crept up a blade of grass and fluttered onto it. We laughed as it meandered over my hand then onto hers. I could hardly breathe thinking about the symbolism and what the ladybird's presence might mean…

"I want to kiss you," came out of nowhere. She leaned forward and kissed me on the cheek.

And *I want to kiss you* was what I wanted to say back to her but of course, I didn't. In matters of love, I never said what I meant. Instead, I said, "Well that's very sweet and I think Jim may have something to say about it!" I let go of her hand, "I think I should clear up the plates."

Louisa grabbed the plates, "I help you. I think I scare you?"

"No, I'm fine, really." I lied. I could never tell her how I really felt about her, how damn tortured I was.

When she left she climbed onto her bike, ruffled my hair and smiled that carefree smile, "See you Saturday."

She didn't. I knew I could never go back. No more cycling for me. It was too dangerous, I wasn't strong enough. I watched her as she cycled into the distance. I held back the tears until she was out of sight. That was why that night in particular, I sobbed uncontrollably in Jim's arms. He could never know.

# CHAPTER TWELVE

ignored Louisa's calls. I never saw her again. I had done her a kindness. The demons would not be allowed to win. I've often thought of the toll on my heart of all the love rejected, the women who I loved and who loved me, but were cast aside in favour of "normalcy."

My head pounded with the self-analysis. There had to be a way through this. *God makes a way where there is no way* was written on the front page of my well-worn journal. But the Bible verse that had opened the door to Christianity was still my mantra, "You shall know the truth, and the truth will set you free." What **was** the truth? And was my truth in direct conflict to God's truth? And is that how the demons got in? To say I was tormented was an understatement. If I couldn't learn to love a man then was I really damned to be lonely forever? The thoughts grew darker. What would be the point of living a lonely life? That thought was an echo of my childhood. If I followed that thread back then maybe I could untangle all this torture? The conclusion I reached was: I had "gay" feelings because I was broken. If I got fixed, then my heart would open to men and the feelings I had for Louisa and countless other women would dissipate and be transferred to the man in my life. I had to keep seeking and praying for healing. I wasn't gay. I couldn't and wouldn't be gay. If only the church approved of therapy—they said it would take me away from God. I had to do this alone, prayer and fasting, more Bible study, service, and staying away from friendships with women, the ones I felt drawn to at least. I would starve it out. It's exactly what I had done with Mother. Starved her out, insulated myself from her warmth in order to protect myself from her cruelty. That plan had worked. It would work again. What was that plan again? I'm rambling. It's amazing that I can even string a sentence together.

My mind was tangled like a vine clinging to a wall for as long as I can remember. I suspect that writing this, is part of the disentangling. The truth that was going to set me free came so gradually and had many reversals. The rejection of my sexuality was not just because it was the most awful thing to be gay, but because I convinced myself that it wasn't my truth. I was damaged and therefore so was my sexual orientation. I had to dedicate my life to healing myself which would undo this perverse way of relating. I was looking for love from a woman because I had not found it with my mother. It all made sense.

Sometimes being with Jim felt like my only choice, like part of some divine curriculum. At the school Christmas party, I was irritated by him. His positivity and uncomplicated love for me felt alienating. My lack of genuine sexual interest in him made me resent him. Sure we had sex, Christian sex, thank God! He was gentle and could turn me on. Also in his favour, he would make the best father to my children. At the Christmas party, my underlying feelings or lack of them came to the fore. We were at a friend's house, in front of the drinks table,

"Claire, can I get you a drink? What would you like?" he asked. His niceness was annoying me.

I tried to dredge up some warmth, and without even thinking said, "Umm, a glass of red?"

"Are you sure you wouldn't like champagne?" He responded—after all, that was my usual.

That triggered the violence in my mind and a silent, 'Why doesn't he just fucking go away? Champagne, red wine? Who gives a fuck?!' I tried not to sneer at him, but I could feel the anger rising. What came out was an icy, "Champagne would be lovely, thank you." My tone was dead and polite and I sounded like my mother. He did a double-take, the chill was visceral.

He put the glass down and firmly said, "I'm taking you home."

"But we've only been here five minutes!" I was shocked. It was a fancy dress party. I was wearing a full-length gold lamé gown, I was a French can-can dancer. He looked dashing in a wide-brimmed hat as a Mexican mariachi. It had taken us ages to get ready.

"What do you mean, you're taking me home?"

"I'm taking you home, I don't want to spend my evening with someone who doesn't want to be with me, doesn't even seem to like me." It wasn't his first experience of this. Up until now, he had tolerated the cold-shouldering but not tonight. He took me by the arm and led me out into the crisp night air. He opened the car door for me and waited for me to climb in. I wanted him to slam the door and be angry but he wasn't and didn't. I didn't fight it because it was all true. I didn't want to be with him. I wanted to be with Louisa. Tears fell down my cheeks, but he had seen enough of those. He didn't relent. His hat got knocked off his head as he got into the driving seat to drive me home.

"Are you going back to the party?" I whimpered.

"Yes, I've been looking forward to it. It won't be the same without you but I can't be with you when you're like this." His eyes were misting up.

"I'm really sorry I'm like this." I managed to say it without self-pity. I meant it.

"I know." He put his hand on my arm, "Sometimes I worry about you Claire, about whether you can ever be truly happy."

When he left I collapsed, sobbing into my brown fake leather couch. Even in sadness and pain, he was chivalrous, and I am driving him away and he's right, I can never be happy. I spent the night, fully clothed, on the sofa; it was comforting to be uncomfortable. I didn't deserve to sleep in a bed. I lay thinking about mother and her cold-shouldering and how it had all but broken my heart and soul. It was a punishment of the cruelest kind. And now I was doing it to Jim and he had only ever been loving to me. He had had enough, the exact same way I had had enough of my mother.

When I look back at my childhood, I am barely able to dredge up the freeze that took place in our home for as long as I can remember. Standing in the small chilly kitchen, unable to remember the crime, shifting from one foot to the other, waiting to be helpful, unable to find a chink in the coldness through which I could be reinstated, made visible again. I wanted to carry the plates, lay the table, wipe the table, put away the mats, tidy the kitchen, be cheerful, say something interesting, make a stunning discovery, give a useful reminder, find lost keys, vacuum before the day it was due, bring in the washing, scowl at my brother's bad behaviour, disapprove of my friends, disown my likes and dislikes, make myself nothing, make myself invisible whilst being useful all at the same time.

I didn't always attempt to make a dent in her coldness because sometimes the freeze was so fierce that to do so would send her deeper into it. She would smell the fear and would feel honor-bound to maintain and intensify the punishment. She knew that my panic created a whirlwind of frenzy and alertness to her needs. The greater the sense of abandonment in me the more I learned to disguise it. I began to train myself to appear nonchalant and indifferent. The effort was superhuman. It took its toll until one day, aged twelve, I made a vow. I vowed that I would never, ever again allow myself to be affected by my mother's coldness and I deduced that the way to do that was to never allow myself to be affected either positively or adversely by her mood whatever that mood might be. The downside of my plan was that my mother was capable of extraordinary warmth and light-heartedness. She would fling her arms around me and squeeze me tight, "Come here you little monkey!" and plant a great big kiss on my cheek. It was manna from heaven, those moments, but in order to insulate myself from the inevitable iciness, I knew that I had to sacrifice the warmth. It was a momentous decision and a long time coming. When it came, it came in a flash. I knew what I had to do. I had no alternative. Separation from my mother's love had to happen for my own sanity. It was survival. I started to feel some control and that felt good and as I absented myself, I felt her loving attempts to regain my devotion. I feared some days that I would crumble under the barrage of her renewed affection, and I was weak from loneliness and starvation. I missed, no, craved those moments of tenderness. I can feel that deprivation now and I can feel the fissure that zigzagged its way across my emotional landscape. The "fault" was there below the earth's surface and its rumblings could be felt for miles and years...

As I dropped off to sleep on the sofa after the short-lived Christmas party, I wondered how I could hold onto Jim. And I wondered if it was even fair to do so. Then, out of nowhere, along came Mary, delivered to us by Mikey.

# CHAPTER THIRTEEN

Mikey, a thirteen-year-old scrawny waif in Jim's class was a resident, with his mother, of the "battered wives" home. At morning registration one day he begged Jim, "Sir, can I have your phone number?"

"Get outta here, Mikey!" was Jim's response.

"Sir! Really Sir! Please give me your number!"

"Mikey, you know I can't give you my number."

"Aw, come on, Sir!"

"All right. Here you go Mikey—you gotta pen? Write this down: 123456789."

"Aw, Sir! Don't be funny, Sir."

"Mikey, I can't give you my number! And what do you want it for anyway?"

"Sir, you gotta give me your number! There's this woman come in the middle of the night, she's come all the way from Dublin, she's got three little kids Sir, and she's got no money. She's got nuffink Sir, and she don't know noone, Sir, and 'er old man tried to kill 'er and I told her you would help 'er, Sir."

"Well, I can't, Mikey."

"Sir, but I told her you would, Sir!"

"Sorry Mikey, I'm here to help you and the kids at the school and I can't be helping every Tom, Dick, and Harry who turns up on your doorstep. That's the social services' job."

"Yeah, woteva." Crestfallen, Mikey left the classroom

and pushed against the flow of kids who were leaving mine. "Miss, can I talk to you?"

Jim had been watching him leave his room, "Oy Mikey, get to your lesson, I'll speak to Miss Goodwin, all right? Now leave it alone."

Angry muttering from Mikey.

During the break, we sat on the beat-up sofa in the staff-room. Jim was wrestling with Mikey's mission, "I can't go and meet some random woman in the battered wives' home for God's sake. Being a bloke, they won't even let me in."

He was right of course. We sat sipping the scalding chipped mugs of coffee. It cost twenty pence, and we never had time to drink it.

Our struggle in letting go of this particular dilemma was that we had never seen Mikey fired up about anything, really, anything. He was one of those pale, thin, undernourished loners who mostly looked vacant, and rarely interacted with other kids, except when he was being bullied, which was most days. So, we were defenseless against his red-faced caring for a complete stranger. It was just too compelling, moving almost. Mikey had found someone less fortunate than himself and he was damned if he wasn't going to help them.

The coffee was particularly rancid that day and we only had five minutes left of break. We had to think fast.

"Well you can't give him your number," I conceded, "but here's an idea. How about I go to the battered wives' home and give her the number of that nice priest at your church? If she's from Dublin, she's probably a Catholic, right?"

"Yeah, but I really don't know if we should be getting involved. Before you know it, we'll have all the kids at school making up some story, and we'll be doing home visits forever!"

But the plan was hatched and Mikey, at afternoon registration, looked as if he had died and gone to heaven. His clenched knuckles were white and his face twisted up into something like a grin. "Thanks, Miss, but you 'ave to come as well Sir 'cos I told 'er you would, and you're my teacher and she won't be expecting Miss."

Children were always thinking up schemes to get us to their homes, as much as they were always trying to get us together. On Valentine's Day, we had both found anonymous cards on our desks with instructions to go to the car park at lunchtime. We of course knew what was afoot but it was far too much fun not to play along. We feigned shock and delight as we discovered each other and forty or so kids poured out from behind the cars, "Caught ya! KISS HER! KISS HER!" they chanted, pointing and laughing. They loved our love for each other. When Jim grabbed me around the waist and planted a kiss on my lips, the cheer that went up from the children sounded like a goal being scored at Wembley Stadium.

So that day after school, guided by a jubilant Mikey, Jim and I drove his tiny white Fiat across the city. The battered wives' home as it happened, was a big regency villa adjacent to my own street. We were practically neighbours. Jim waited in the car. As I approached the house I wondered what I would find. Mikey was beaming, sort of. He let me in through the shabby brown door and knocked on an internal door marked Room 2. The noise within of small children's voices was deafening as they threw themselves at the door. A young Irishwoman's voice could be heard over the din. "Kids get away from the door and shut up!"

Mary was clearly no weakling and smiled warmly as she let me in. She was my age, blonde curly hair, strong and outgoing. Only her broad Irish accent set us apart. We sat on the sofa and she explained that she was through with her husband's alcoholic rages and knife-to-the-throat scenes in front of her three, five, and seven-year-old children. "The three-year-old," she went on, "has taken to wandering around the streets, knocking on complete stranger's doors, and asking if she can live with them!"

While we chatted, a scruffy boy, the oldest, kept the two girls in check as they bounced on the double bed. It was the only bed in the room. Their tumbling curls and big anxious eyes, sent my plan to send her to the priest, out of the window.

"What are you doing about dinner, Mary?" I asked.

"Well, as you can see, we are bouncing off the walls in here and it's extremely kind of you to come and see us. I don't want to put you to any trouble. The kids think they're on their holidays and I'm just happy to be away from that brute! That's all I care about. We had to hide in the docks till midnight for the ferry to leave in case my husband got wind of it. I waited for him to pass out cold from the booze, and then I ran with the kids to the neighbours'. I'd already hid a bag in the bushes. It was her that drove us to the ferry. I tried to run away once before but he found us and it wasn't pretty, so I thought I'd try putting some water between us. It's been a long time coming." She spoke with urgency, as if she were still running.

Jim was typically unphased when, a few moments later, we emerged and all five of us somehow climbed into his car. The small boy went in the boot and Mary sat jammed in the backseat with the two girls. Mikey waved us off triumphantly as we chugged off down the road and round the corner to my house.

Lots of tea, and bread and jam later, the kids were relieved to be running around the garden. I found myself glancing over at Jim and Mary who were sitting on the threadbare lawn, deep in conversation, they were oblivious to what was going on around them. Something was happening. They had barely touched their tea. They had the same blonde curly hair, the same easy laugh. I was like a forensic scientist analyzing clues after a collision with a psychic truck.

We drove them home, happy and fed. I was wrestling inside with how much I needed this man and what I had just seen. The kids changed down to their undergarments and they all climbed into the big bed. I sat Mary down on the sofa and once again Jim waited outside. I felt as if I were plotting my own demise. "Mary," I whispered, "forgive me for being so direct, but what do you think of Jim?"

"He's fantastic, never met a bloke like him and he's so good looking! I mean, what I mean is..." she coloured up, "He's your boyfriend for Christ's sake! What the hell am I saying?"

That was all I needed, "Well I know this sounds strange because we only just met but I feel like I need to tell you something. Jim and I are together but the truth is, I'm never going to marry him and I think he might like you and I just want you to know that it's ok with me if you like him."

She looked aghast. The psychic truck had now reached her and as she tried to hold back her tears she grabbed both my hands, "Thank you, Claire. I have no idea what you just said or why the hell you are saying it, but you must be out of your bloody mind!"

We hugged, "Jim and I will pick you up Saturday," I said, and we will all go out to Purley Castle. The kids will love it, there's lots of ruins and grass to run in and I'll keep an eye on them while you spend some time with Jim."

"I don't know what just happened," she blubbered, "but I've been praying for a miracle for years. I think you might be an angel sent by God." With her lilting Irish accent, that sounded entirely plausible, but the truth was, I too had been praying and it occurred to me that maybe she was my angel sent by God. She was the answer to *my* prayers.

It took no longer than a five-minute whispered conversation for my life to be upended. I went out to the car to complete the final stage of this drastically revised plan. "Jim, what did you think?" I said, as he started up the engine.

"What did I think about what?"

"What did you think about Mary?"

"Well, she seemed very nice. What are you asking me that for?"

"I think something happened back there in the garden."

"In the garden? We had a cup of tea and a sandwich, and I love your mum's strawberry jam." He was being his usual jokey self.

"Something happened." I hesitated, disbelieving, but resolute.

"I think you fell in love with Mary. I saw it happen. And I think she fell in love with you."

I needed no confirmation but the awkward silence followed by an involuntary tear trickling down this tough northern man's left cheek was shocking. I had never seen him like this. I went on, "You even look the same, you talk the same, and you could almost be related!" I stuttered, choked back the tears, in awe of what was happening.

Silence.

"What about you? Us?" he asked, bewildered. He wasn't denying it.

"What about me? I've messed you around for long enough. I love you, Jim. You're the kindest man I know but I know that I will never marry you. "

Silence again as we pulled up outside my house.

"She's got three kids," he protested. Right there I knew it was perfect.

"Jim, you've always wanted to adopt or open your own children's home. This *is* your dream. You *told* me you wanted to adopt children as well as having your own. And these kids come without paperwork—they're a bonus!"

There was nothing he could say.

He walked me to my door.

"Don't come in," I said, "I'll see you at school tomorrow." I kissed him on the cheek. He reached out and held me, the strong arms, the rough stubble against my face, the smell of him, his curls tickling my ear. I was crumbling and wanted to sob but it wasn't the time. The sky had turned red and orange as he turned and walked back to the car. Rooted in the doorway watching his car disappear down the road, I cried and held onto the feeling that I had done something good. I had set him free.

We spent that Saturday at the castle and I knew it would be our last outing, a surreal handover of a truly beautiful man to a truly beautiful woman. I stalked them over the next few weeks, sitting outside his apartment in my car just to get a glimpse of him. I wanted to turn back the clock. I hadn't expected the grief to hit so hard. Without his warmth, I was in a void, a black hole. I tried being friends with them but none of us could stand it. It had happened so quickly that adjusting seemed impossible.

Sitting in the car in the cold outside his flat was when the idea of going back to missionary work came to my rescue. Being in an adjacent classroom to him was intolerable. I didn't tell him that nearly all the time that I was with him, I had been thinking about Louisa. He deserved more. I must end this and devote myself to God. I wondered if I looked hard enough and far afield enough, I might find a real cure, but in the meantime, I was glad that I was no longer deceiving him. I couldn't break any more hearts. I must dedicate myself to a solitary spiritual calling.

Over the next few weeks, I searched and searched and came across an organization called Youth with a Mission. They had centres worldwide. I felt drawn to Amsterdam and Ontario, Canada. The Canadian base was renowned for its deep healing work. A minister that I confided in said that they would both be good options given my "psychological problem." I longed to return to the simplicity of my spiritual path.

In the autumn half-term holiday, I flew to Amsterdam. I stayed there for five nights, joining in the activities and outreach to the community. On the last night, I was having dinner with the members of a South African gospel band and I was dreading going back to England and my classroom next to Jim. A decision had to be made. I couldn't decide between Canada and Amsterdam,

I said to Johann, the lead vocalist of the band, "I'm going to the bathroom and when I come back I will have a decision." I made my way to the bathroom at the back of the restaurant. I sat on the seat of the toilet, and put my head in my hands and prayed. I felt nothing. I heard nothing. Disappointed, I stood up. I was no nearer knowing where to go. My eyes landed on the only graffiti on the back of the door, in big bold letters, it said, "With love from Ontario Canada."

I smiled a big smile of relief. There it was. I went back to the table and my new friends were delighted for me,

"Don't you just love it," said Johann, laughing "when the writing is literally on the wall!"

So I rented out my house, and I arrived in London, Ontario in deep snow. I had never seen so much snow. My new friends were warm and mostly Canadian and I felt sure that help was on the way.

I found out, eight months after my departure, that Mary had given birth, and she and Jim were married shortly after that. They had two more children and Jim remained at the school. He supported Mary, who had been training for the Olympic swimming squad when she fell pregnant in Ireland for the first time. Jim got her back into training and she qualified yet again, this time for the UK veterans' swimming squad. Jim's first gift to me had been a pair of Nike's—*that* was the difference between Mary and me. She probably wore hers.

# CHAPTER FOURTEEN

"Hey guys, remember that Mary gave birth to Jesus in a stable surrounded by farmyard animals? Donkeys and sheep? It stank! She's exhausted but she knows this is God's baby. You have to move like you know you're carrying the Saviour of the world! I want more!" That was Greg, our handsome American director. He had once appeared in a musical on Broadway.

We were at the Ontario Christian Performing Arts Missionary School, auditioning for a mimed presentation of the gospel. The role we were trying out for was the Virgin Mary. I was gliding and floating and gazing dreamily up at the sky but rapidly running out of inspiration.

Joe, a bodybuilder from Chicago, growled as he glided by me, arms outstretched, "I pray I don't get this part!"

"Me neither," I whispered back.

Rich, the son of a prairie ranch owner, on the other side of the gym, took the instructions more literally. He was reenacting Jesus' birth, legs akimbo, panting loudly.

"Okay guys, great job, let's move on," Greg said.

Seated in the front row of the empty auditorium, three of the missionary leaders were scrutinizing our every move and scribbling on clipboards.

"The music will change now," Greg said, "and we want your best version of Satan. Ready. GO!"

Creepy cello music kicked in. Playing Satan was more fun, it came more naturally. As I was writhing around on the ground, thinking evil thoughts, I glanced across the room at Andrea, a young woman doing split jumps and ballet moves. She was clearly a trained ballerina. She flicked her hair back and glared at me. I knew I had to keep writhing in the opposite direction. I must stay away from her. But then she came spinning and swirling around me, hissing, "Come on Englishwoman, you can do better than that!" I lunged forward as if to attack and she winked, "That's better!"

After we finished being Satan, we moved onto Adam, Eve, Jesus, Joseph, the angels, the wise men, and finally the shepherds. Greg eventually called out, "Okay guys, free time now. We'll let you know our decision after supper."

I grabbed my puffer jacket, put on my snow boots, and crunched through the deep snow back to the dormitory. I felt an arm slip through mine. It was Andrea. I felt a rush, then terror. I didn't squeeze her arm back, I acted casual, I mustn't encourage her. She was undeterred.

"This is hilarious, right?" she said laughing, pulling me around to make eye contact.

"Most fun I've ever had..." I sounded sarcastic, trying to be cool, so I followed up with, "No really, it was fun." I was embarrassed.

"Ha! You don't do "sincere" do you, Goodwin! I like that. You're so English!"

Don't do sincere? I suppose not. I had to think about it.

After supper, perched on the trestle tables in the canteen, we awaited our fate. They went through the list of twenty-four roles, calling out our names. It was thrilling. I wore leggings and legwarmers for the occasion. I was living the dream, *Fame*, the Christian version. Here I could use my love of performing without being found out. I had always longed to go to acting school but I knew it meant kissing people, which, outside of marriage, the church disapproved of. And I knew I might fall for a girl and I would have to be honest about my feelings and that would mean being found out.

There were only three roles left and I had not yet been allocated a role. Neither had Andrea. The suspense was killing us.

"Andrea, you are our Virgin Mary. Your dancing is such a joy. We've decided that you will also double up as Eve." The director beamed at her. Huge round of applause.

"Matty, you are going to be playing the roles of Jesus and Joseph, you know, because we don't have enough men. And finally, the main role goes to Claire. Claire, your depiction of Satan was utterly compelling. Congratulations!" Huge cheer. He continued, "We will be devoting extra prayer to Claire because her role comes with a certain level of danger. Our past two Satan's both ran into life-threatening situations. One of them was in a near-fatal car accident and almost lost the use of her legs, and the other one suffered major depression and psychological difficulties as a result of playing this part. We chose you, Claire, because we felt that you were spiritually strong enough to cope, but you might want to think about it before you commit? Let us know by tomorrow because the three of you need to start rehearsing together."

Playing the part of Satan really didn't faze me. I already possibly had twelve demons that they didn't know about and I seemed to be doing fine with them. Moreover, the idea of rehearsing with Andrea clinched it for me. I had tried really hard to avoid her and now God was *forcing* us together. It was a green light.

"I don't think I need to think about it. I'll be fine." I felt a little smug, knowing how well I was coping with demon possession. To be honest, I wasn't completely sure anymore about the demons, whether they even existed.

With only three weeks to prepare, Andrea and I did indeed spend a great deal of time together. I was taught basic jiu-jitsu and opened the show with high kicks and punching. The temptation of Eve was the first scene, the music was alternately bombastic and creepy. I prowled around Andrea aka Eve, like a slimy snake and then intimidated her by kicking her in the face, only narrowly missing her.

"It has to be realistic," urged the director, "so you have to almost skim her face."

Privately Andrea protested, "Surely you don't have to kick that close?!"

I didn't know what to say, except that I would be careful. I didn't find it easy, re-enacting a seduction that was going on in my mind, both on, and off the stage. It reinforced on a daily basis how rotten I was inside. Maybe that is how Satan would get me, by whispering in my ear, day and night, how evil I was, till I could bear it no longer? I noticed how the other performers seemed to be backing away from me. Maybe they sensed my true nature.

At the dress rehearsal, Andrea wore a pretty fitted blue dress which showed off her ballet dancer figure and I was clad in a sinister black stretch jumpsuit with silver sequins. The elaborate face paint took over two hours to apply, shiny silver on one side, and gold on the other: the two sides of Satan, the fallen angel. That was me. I kept the crushing fear of destruction to myself. It was alleviated by the comfort of Andrea's warmth, her humour, and friendship. We rehearsed all day, every day, except Sundays of course. Our mission destination was kept a secret until only a few weeks before departure. It would be either Hawaii, Honduras, or Philadelphia. Of course, we all wanted Hawaii and none of us wanted to go to Philadelphia or Honduras. I wasn't entirely convinced of the usefulness of going to Hawaii or Philadelphia but apparently, they needed to hear about Jesus there as much as anywhere. The group outing to the clinic for hepatitis, tetanus, and tuberculosis jabs eliminated Philadephia we thought, though without Google in those days, we were in the dark.

"The moment you have all been waiting for!" said Greg. It was breakfast, the temperature inside was not much higher than outside and I was bundled up in my padded waterproof jacket and woolly bobble hat. I just wanted to feel warm again, so when Greg announced, "We leave for Honduras in two weeks!" I was overjoyed, it would be hot there. Hawaii had sounded exotic but in all honesty, my only real barometer was how close I could be to Andrea. Nothing else mattered.

Our first 'practice' performance was local: Toronto Maximum Security Prison. Being in prisons was not unfamiliar to me. I had previously taught Italian to an IRA bomber at Long Lartin prison in the UK, so I wasn't overly intimidated by the intense security, double air locking doors, or the sounds of the prisoners catcalling from their cells. In the Toronto prison, when it came to perform, our leader gathered us to pray.

*Fiona Goodwin*

"Lord, these are dangerous men, protect us and bless us. Bless the guards and may they turn their gaze away as we reach out to the prisoners to bring them your love. Okay, kids, we have been told it's not safe to leave the stage but this is too good an opportunity, so, as soon as the performance ends, everyone who is brave enough, should go down and talk to the prisoners. Ask God who you should reach out to."

It sounded exciting! Breaking the rules for God! Saving souls! As Satan, I felt that I should lead the charge. As the closing music died, I headed down the center aisle to the back of the auditorium into a sea of three hundred men. There was one man I wanted to talk to who was at the back. He was glad to talk. He had just started reading the Bible, he wanted God in his life. I prayed with him. Then a nervous guard shouted, "Block B return to your cells!" and off they went.

It was exhilarating, sharing the gospel with a man who wanted to hear. I so desperately wanted to do something brave and good. Greg complimented me on setting an example to the team, "We definitely made the right choice when we picked you to be Satan! Great job out there today!"

It was soon time to load our luggage onto the top of the yellow school bus to embark on a ten-day journey down through Canada, America to New Orleans, where we would fly to Honduras.

It was only natural that Andrea and I would sit next to each other on the bus because we had now become insepa-rable, spending so much time in rehearsal together. Satan and Mary and Eve were mostly in the same scenes, we were only occasionally joined by Jesus/Joseph. As we all bundled onto the bus, I was horrified to see little Judy Sarcora low-ering herself into the seat next to Andrea. Andrea looked up at me and apologetically shrugged her shoulders. I was beside myself with rage and disappointment. How dare she? She was just one of the shepherds and she barely knew Andrea. To be honest, she barely knew anyone. She was a nobody who just kept hanging around Andrea. Shutting out the excitement of my fellow travellers, I sat on my own and silently sulked all the way to the next truck stop. I couldn't look at Andrea. I turned my rage inwards and berated myself for my mean, unchristian behaviour. I was a jealous, messed up, no-good whack job who didn't deserve to be on this planet, let alone on this bus! Spreading the message of Christ! What a joke! I pretended to be asleep for the rest of the day. Following that, Andrea and I became experts at anticipating the jostling for position, always making sure we climbed on the bus together and then averted our eyes if it looked like someone was trying to connect with us. With this strategy, we always ended up sitting together.

Snuggling close in a haze of happiness, we watched Canada and America fly by. Iconic names that we recognised from the movies—Lake Erie, Detroit, Toledo, Dayton, Cincinnati, Louisville, Nashville, Birmingham. I wanted to hold Andrea's hand of course, but falling asleep on her shoulder was almost as good. I didn't want to scare her off and she liked boys after all. Having said that, it was confusing how much she wanted to be with me, how tactile and affectionate she was. I had to remind myself, I'm here to be cured but I was in a constant state of longing. My heart beat so loud I thought it would be heard above the roar of the ancient bus. I had started the training by rededicating myself to having only 'pure' relationships. I needed to succeed. I thought of Jim and how much stronger my feelings were for Andrea. And then I thought about Louisa and the kiss after the bike ride. And of course, there was Lydia, my first kiss. The further south we travelled, the more terrifying were the roadside billboards:

"'HELL IS REAL!'
HOMOSEXUALITY IS AN ABOMINATION.
TEL 855-FOR-TRUTH!"

# CHAPTER FIFTEEN

"Plantain and rice" I sighed, "Yum! This makes a change!" I said it sarcastically under my breath just after the twenty-eight of us had sung, "Thank you thank you Jesus!" I didn't know what plantain was before Honduras. They look like big bananas but taste disappointingly like a potato. We all sat around on the dirt floor outside the church hall where we were staying. One by one, we went up to a wooden table where a scoop of the sticky rice and plantain was slapped into our bowls. The team funds were so meagre that this was considered a big treat after days of peanut butter and jelly sandwiches.

"You better eat it," Andrea said, "and be grateful 'cos that's all you're getting. Let's take ours away from the others." There she goes again, reading my mind, wanting to be alone with me.

We sat under the shade of a coconut palm, and although ravenous, the heavy forkfuls went to our mouths slowly. The tropical rain was about to throw itself down. When it did, we didn't stir. Moments of being alone together were worth the brief drenching.

"Let's pretend it's steak and chips," I said. If only! I thought, "Steak and chips followed by an ice cream sundae with a bottle of wine and then..."

The fantasy was thrilling and dangerous. I was wearing

my Satan suit and Andrea was wearing her Virgin Mary suit. The irony was not lost on me that we were dressed as we were and conducting a clandestine affair as we toured Honduras, preaching the gospel in a missionary team. Clandestine affair? What clandestine affair? We hadn't even kissed, we hadn't even held hands, but in my mind, with my conviction of guilt, and with the terror of the world seeing my true nature, I took sitting next to her in the dirt, eating potato flavoured bananas, as the equivalent of a "clandestine affair," even though absolutely nothing had happened between us, nothing.

I was twenty-eight, Andrea twenty-three, she was strangely worldly and old for her years. Adopted into the wrong family as she put it, her parents were well-meaning fundamentalist Christians. She sang opera and her parents' hobbies were beer, burgers, and church—not to mention the Pat Robertson show on the Christian TV channel that announced the 'good news' twenty-four seven.

"Book learnin' is for folks that don't do a decent day's work. The Bible is the only book you should be readin'." According to Andrea, that was her mother's neat summary of what we all needed to be doing.

What I really needed to be doing was rescuing the Virgin Mary. One night our "affair" dramatically shifted from fantasy to reality. We were in the mountains in the rain forest, in the village of Choloma, reputedly the centre for witchcraft for the whole of Honduras. Following the evening performance, we were all getting ready to settle down to sleep on the hard floor of the school hall, our temporary home. Some were already sleeping, twenty-eight of us lay in rows, elbow to elbow. I was still in my Satan suit. I was just looking for my toothbrush when I heard a piercing scream coming from the outhouse. It was Andrea. My heart stopped. I grabbed my torch and ran out into the blackness, to rescue her. The vegetation was tall and thick and I found her, still in her Virgin Mary suit, pinned against the back wall of the outhouse. She was sobbing and screaming and pointing—at a tarantula! I couldn't believe my luck! With one fell swoop, I grabbed the mop and flicked the furry creature away. Andrea threw herself into my arms. She asked if she could stay with me. I said, "Of course! I'll take you back inside." She clung onto me as I lead her back to the schoolhouse. Feeling her pounding heart against my chest and her arms so fiercely wrapped around me felt unlike anything I had ever experienced. I never wanted to let her go. I didn't want to return to the team's sleeping area. I wanted to be alone with her. We passed the door to the geography room. I tried the handle. It opened and in we went and there we turned and faced each other and amongst the globes and maps of the world, the dam burst. We hungrily found each other's mouths and kissed. Months of longing and restraint were over as we wrestled our love into existence on the hard floor under the teacher's wooden desk. We were Satan and Mary—and we were both going to hell. I was overjoyed and devastated simultaneously. This was not what was meant to happen. This was where I had come to be cured! I was back to square one, which for me was Dante's second circle of hell.

Every day in our performance, I had to writhe around and deceive Eve and then plot to bring about the death of Jesus until, at the end of the show, Jesus would pin me down and the show would end with his foot on my head. As the music rose to a crescendo, I was banished forever into

*Fiona Goodwin*

the flames of hell! Every night that we made love, I knew that my soul was descending into the abyss. I was deliriously happy and the most depressed I had ever been. My thoughts turned to ending my life. Shouldn't I love Andrea enough to release her and spare her damnation? I can't be responsible for taking her down with me. I should spare everyone. If it wasn't Andrea, there could be other women who I might lead astray.

My decision to kill myself was thwarted by the fact that suicide was a sin. I tried to weigh up which was worse, suicide or homosexuality? Maybe sacrificing my life is what I had to do. Andrea, on the other hand, didn't get what the fuss was about. She had been sleeping with boys since she was fourteen. As far as she was concerned, this was the most loving relationship she had ever been in. She was five years younger than me. I was therefore responsible. I decided I wouldn't kill myself (yet) and I wouldn't give her up, not here in the middle of the rain forest of Honduras and in the middle of our missionary tour. My British stance of *Keep Calm and Carry On* came to the fore, I couldn't let the team down.

Most nights we waited till everyone was asleep and crept out to find a hiding place in an empty classroom or closet or office.

"I wonder what it will be like when we don't have to hide from Christians anymore," she said angrily.

"We will still have to hide."

"Sure," she said, "but at least we won't be watched all the time and we won't be sharing a room with twenty-six other people!"

"Hmm, maybe we will miss the intrigue…"

"Like HELL!" she burst out, "Oops! Sorry, Satan!"

"No worries Our Lady—I will have to think of a suitable punishment. I might get one of those coconuts to fall on your head."

She tugged at my Satan cape, "Hmm, I've grown very fond of your punishments—you're going to have to think up some more."

Sometimes we left the building and made out in the dark against the stucco wall, giggling at the strange sounds of the jungle, wondering, but not really caring, if a snake would carry us off. One night we were entwined on the floor of a locked broom cupboard, it was the only privacy we could find. In my torment I attempted to do the right thing, "Don't you worry about what we are doing? About hell?" My face was in the nape of her neck, we were naked.

"What do you mean," she asked, pulling away. I countered with, "Well what it says in the Bible?" She replied, "We just have to keep it a secret, we will never find love like this again, there isn't anyone else I want to be with." She looked so lost and sad.

I reminded her, "But, we have to go back to Canada and I will have to go back to…"

She lost it, sobbing, pushing me away, furious, "Don't fucking do this Goodwin! Don't talk like this! Don't you dare dump me! You can't leave. You made me love you and now you're going to spoil everything and leave?!" She was now in a fetal position, out of control, deep gasps of grief.

"I'm sorry! I'm sorry!" I begged her forgiveness. "I won't talk about it again." I reached out to calm her. She pushed me away again. I started to sob, her rejection was so unspeakably painful. She eventually let me hold her and we cried together on that cold stone floor.

We continued our liaison and I kept unspoken my

conviction that I was eternally damned and that, in this life, and in the afterlife, we could never be together.

At the end of the missionary tour, we were all like school kids let out for summer. I went to stay at Andrea's home in Canada. We lived on her parents' land in a trailer. They had no idea just how bad and wonderful an idea it was to put us alone together. Her father paid me to clean his petrol tanker every day with a hundred-foot industrial hose, every tomboy's dream job, but the knell tolled for us fated lovers. My attempts to get a green card failed, and desolate, I was forced to return to England. The memory of her ashen face at Toronto Airport still haunts me.

Every few days, we sent to each other in the mail, hour-long cassette recordings, of sobbing. She phoned in the middle of the night, threatening to kill herself. She didn't. Instead, she married Rick, the chap who played Jesus/ Joseph, a bipolar drug addict. They had a baby.

Her new husband, had been advised by the church not to seek psychiatric help for his condition. He ended up getting committed for mugging an elderly lady for drug money.

Meanwhile back in London, I was beyond grief-stricken. I was getting reprimanded at my new high school teaching job for poor punctuality. Previously, I had always been conscientious and professional, but I was falling apart. I decided I had to ignore the terrifying warnings from the church that I would lose my faith if I went to a therapist. I had nothing to live for. I prayed, "God, as I am, I am no good to you, I am a mess, always heartbroken. I've tried doing it your way but I haven't been cured and now I have to risk losing you too. I'm going to get professional help. I'm done with all the Christians praying for me. God, if you are the loving God that I think you are, and if I go into therapy and we part company, I think you will understand." I wept bitterly but there was some relief that I was going to find a new kind of help.

At the local mental health clinic, I arrived for my first appointment with Dr. Neil Mackey. He was only a little older than me, disheveled, wearing a beaten-up corduroy jacket. His hair was uncombed and possibly unwashed. I took a deep breath and shaking inside, I launched into, "I think I might be… bisexual." It sounded better than "gay." I awaited the horrified reaction. None came.

"You know Claire, it's okay to be bisexual or gay," his voice was kind.

It's okay for you to say, I thought. I struggled to trust him, he wasn't a Christian. He didn't know about hell and the second coming and the fact that dinosaurs and evolution were all made up. After my ten allocated sessions, I was deemed to be no longer at risk, but I was still determined to be straight. I still couldn't face the shame of being gay and I certainly didn't want to be alone.

The pain, however, of maintaining the tenuous thread with Andrea, thousands of miles away, just became a cruel reminder that we would never be together. We decided in one agonised 3 a.m. phone call to break off all contact so that we could heal and start our lives afresh.

I had gone to Canada to get over Jim and I returned to England to get over Andrea. It was a disaster! All of my community were Christians so I continued to attend church and Bible study because that was where my friends were, but my heart wasn't in it. I felt myself slipping away, my fervour was gone and I was a shell. It had happened, I was losing my faith in God.

# CHAPTER SIXTEEN

T he devastation of no longer having Andrea in my life, would not stop hemorrhaging. For a fleeting moment, I had tasted the sweetness of waking each morning to being held, skin on skin. I had known the anticipation of intimacy, night after night.

Before long, I was unable to walk but a few steps. Glandular fever led to a compromised immune system, which led to hepatitis B and finally, a tiredness in my bones and my core that made eating an almost insurmountable chore. I was diagnosed with post-viral fatigue syndrome and M.E. I became dangerously thin, skeletal even. Antibiotics were no longer effective. Even a bad flu could be life-threatening. I had a glimpse of what it would be like to lose my home, my livelihood. I felt the isolation that comes from being immobile and too tired for even the briefest conversation. With my physical wellbeing under siege, staying alive was the priority. I knew I was slipping away. My body's inertia gave me permission to go inward, I went back into therapy, this time with a Jungian analyst.

Looking back, I think my body was tired of the lie, tired of not being touched, tired of hopelessness. The professional long-term therapy that had been denied me by the church leaders, started to do its work: the fear of damnation lessened, compassion for myself and curiousity about life replaced the narrow existence of fundamentalism. The idea that only born again Christians were to be trusted, also dissipated. The most terrifying thing of all was knowing that questioning all of this would put me outside of the only community I knew. Who would I be without this purpose to save souls? What could possibly be as meaningful? How would I fit into society? I had become ignorant only reading the Bible and Christian literature. I had eliminated friendships with anyone outside the church. Gradually, and not without trepidation, I opened to the possibility of a new life. In the words of Mary Oliver:

"Determined to do
The only thing you could do.
Determined to save
The only life you could save."

With this permission, I began to indulge my love of television and films. I felt guilty at first, enjoying them so much, and guilty that I was doing that instead of studying the Bible. Over eighteen months church meetings were replaced by videos from Blockbusters. I studied calligraphy, devoting hours to refining the shape of each character. I battled the gnawing feeling that I wasn't doing anything important or useful.

Each day, physically, I could make one journey down the sixteen stairs to the sitting room and then one journey back up at night. For breakfast, I was able to stand in the kitchen to boil a kettle and while it boiled. I would lean both elbows on the counter to find the strength to tear off the corner of a packet of powdered chicken soup (the only thing my stomach would allow) and tip it into a mug and then stir in the water with the spoon, trying to remove the lumps. I rinsed the spoon immediately under the tap so that it would be clean and ready for use for the next meal, and then I would go through the same process in the evening. On days when my body felt strong enough, I would pour the boiling water onto egg noodles and then return to the sofa to watch them soften in the bowl and become digestible for my weary stomach. My digestive system was shutting down, refusing to participate. Too much energy was required to go through these rituals and I wondered if my system might shut down completely. I'm not sure how much I cared if it did. My interest in staying alive, however, was gaining strength and along with it, my mind and body. After nearly two years, I went back to work full-time.

# CHAPTER SEVENTEEN

hat's when Alexandra showed up.

I was thirty-two, she was forty-five. I am afraid to write these words because they will never do justice to her, to us, or to her family who I came to love and who loved me. We promised never to tell a soul. We told each other that it was a story that could never be told, but here I am telling it.

We met in an airless, windowless, dusty storeroom at a high school in London where I taught French and where she had arrived, having just been appointed head of the department.

Her black leather handbag remained strapped across her chest over a black wool cape and then, as the room warmed up with all twelve members of the department cramped around a small table, she removed the bag and cape to reveal a figure-hugging brown flecked herringbone skirt that went below the knee and a wide brown leather belt over a thin cashmere fawn sweater. Her flat ankle boots were crumpled soft tan leather over ribbed woolen tights. She was addressing a disparate bunch, the antithesis of a team, and she breathed life into us with her every word *and* with the *pain auchocolat* and the big urn of coffee that she poured into plastic cups. The free cup of coffee got our attention but even more so the pain au chocolat! We

LOVED free stuff. I don't recall much of what she talked about, I just remember how she made me feel. She seemed to like us and spoke glowingly about her love of teaching as if it were something worthwhile and fun.

"I'm so grateful to be here," she said, "this is a very forward-thinking school and I'll be making some changes. You're clearly all very competent and dedicated, but operating under challenging circumstances. The state and age of the text books is unacceptable," she waved a book with no cover and ripped corners, "we will be getting new ones that we will decide on together. And the fact that you appear to have only one board marker per classroom is untenable. More importantly, I think you will agree, morale is low, so we are all going to have the day off on Wednesday to go off-site to a local hotel—a four-course lunch will be provided. So leave your packed lunch at home!"

That provoked sharp intakes of breath from everyone. A day off? Lunch! Unheard of! She also planned to paint walls and buy enough board markers, both blue and coloured, for everyone to have their own supply and she was going to meet with us every week to find out our needs.

She closed the meeting with, "I know this job isn't easy. I have children. I know about teenagers! We have to make it fun for them as well as for us!"

Fun? What a concept?! I had only gone into teaching to earn money to get away from home whilst awaiting the launch of my "international preaching ministry." But here was someone enthusing about teaching; she was passionate and I was fascinated.

Alexandra had moved from Bristol to follow her husband, who had taken over a pharmaceutical company in the city. She had a stunning smile and laughed uproariously.

My colleagues and I were both intrigued and inspired. The meeting was short and we spilled out into the drafty corridor. She called me back," Fiona, can I have a word?" I hovered in the doorway, "Certainly."

She continued, "How are you doing? I understand you've had some health issues. We are going to put you in the classroom next to me so that I can keep an eye on you. I don't want to lose you." I was wrapped in that wide smile.

"I'm doing well now thanks, starting to put on weight!" I was grateful to have been singled out.

"I'm also a little confused," she went on, "In the paperwork when I applied for the job you were called Claire, but you were introduced today as Fiona?"

"Ah well, the short version: I was Claire till a few months ago when I changed my name back to Fiona which is actually my first name."

"How intriguing." She said it warmly. "Well, thanks for clearing that up."

I wanted to tell Alexandra the long version but that didn't happen until sometime after that first meeting. This was not the time or the place.

# CHAPTER EIGHTEEN

was thirty-three when I had begun to feel uncomfortable about being called Claire. It came to me at the start of therapy during the worst of the illness. It occurred to me that changing my name back to Fiona could be the key to unlocking something, me perhaps. The unthinkable was pressing on my brain, "Change your name back to Fiona! But only Americans do that sort of thing!" I argued inside myself, "It's self-obsessed, pretentious nonsense. I will not change my name. Claire is a perfectly good name. People will think that I have gone completely mad." But it came in waves like contractions. I tried to stuff it down. A visiting American christian counselor was recommended to me. I made an appointment. She told me that I had SPD, split personality disorder, which only confirmed what I felt about Americans but there was a ring of truth.

"Your sexuality," she said, "got shut down with Fiona when your father left and your mother attempted to destroy the reminder that you were a part of him, you disappeared, you abdicated your own identity to ease your mother's pain, oh and when you had to share her bed, you were her surrogate husband."

I was now all the more convinced that changing my name would be an entirely American thing to do and I resolved to hold out. But the thoughts became a deluge;

they would build and then subside, like something waiting to be born. My resistance got weaker with every new wave, I tried my hardest to head it off, but it wouldn't go away. I surrendered.

Mother did not take it well, "Well darling, I will continue to call you Claire."

"Why is that mum?"

"Because that's your name darling and it's a very pretty name."

"Yes, but wasn't Fiona a pretty name?"

"Don't be facetious. Claire is your name now." She was adamant, she had a tea towel in her hand and was wiping dishes. I tried another tack, "Mum, did you choose the name Claire and Keith chose the name Fiona?"

In front of Mother, I called Dad by his name—it was possibly only the second time I had had the courage to mention him at all since he left when I was five. She blanched, struggled to gain her composure and blurted, "No, we both liked both names, they are both very pretty names." This was the first time I was hearing any parental accord. Calmly and gently I inquired again, "So Mum, why is it so difficult to call me Fiona?"

"It's not darling, I just prefer Claire."

I was losing the fight, getting nowhere. It was a silly idea this name changing and I wanted to drop it but it felt as if I was on to something. I didn't know what it was, and then she gave me the answer. Conspiratorially, she leaned forward and whispered, "You know, Fiona was a very pretty little girl."

I felt as if I had been physically punched. Her tone told me that she was talking about someone who no longer existed, someone who had died. I left the kitchen and stumbled into the garden. I sat on the wrought iron bench because I could no longer stand and because I felt sobs coming up from deep within. Images flashed in front of my eyes: the drastic cutting of my long blond tresses: the pretty dresses turning into dungarees; Mum slipping her engagement ring onto my finger whilst I promised never to marry and never to wear lipstick. I looked like my father, Fiona had been made to vanish. It was making sense. I was grief-stricken but relieved that I had not given up on the girl who had gone missing—she wasn't dead, she had merely gone underground. And now I knew her name and I was calling her back to life. We would be friends—she would forgive me for turning my back on her.

My father reacted nervously when I told him a week or so later. He stuttered, "Why change your name to Fiona, if you want to change your name, fine, but if you want you could pick an entirely different name, any name! Charlotte's a nice name! Why not call yourself Charlotte?"

I didn't argue, "Yes Charlotte is a nice name, but if you don't mind I would like to be called Fiona."

"Hmm, you haven't told your mother have you?"

"Yes I have."

Incredulous, "You haven't, have you?"

There was a hint of admiration. He straightened up. "Wow," and then slowly, "well, I'm sure I can get used to calling you Fiona. Lucy!" he called out to his wife, "Lucy, we are going to call Claire *Fiona* from now on!"

"Great!" She called back from the kitchen, "that's a really nice name!" He smiled at me.

"Thanks, Dad"

"Not at all. It's a lovely day today, would you like to give me a hand getting the cover off the Ferrari? We could take her out for a spin later, how does that sound?"

"Hmm love to, thanks."

"Great! Let's do it!"

"Yes let's!"

Dad was unabashed about his love of Ferraris. Even when he couldn't really afford one he somehow managed always to have one in the dust-proofed garage. I liked that. I loved cars too. Mostly I loved his enthusiasm. When he left us in his late twenties, he too was made to disappear. Mother took all the family cine films and had them doctored to remove footage of him *and* his cars. She hated him and them. Taking me out in the car was how I experienced his affection and, on that particular day, he broke all the speed limits and the roar of that engine felt like the roar of intimacy. So much in a name! I had been Claire for thirty years, devoted to compliance, to mother, and to self-denial.

As for my brothers, Rupert and Christopher were my allies when it came to the change of name. My younger brother Rupert was not yet born on the infamous day of the birthday cake, yet he was the first brave enough to call me Fiona in front of Mother. He fought his own battles. My most vivid memory of his rage was when he was seven. He had lost the dog lead. He was scared of Mother's wrath, streaming with tears, wrestling with guilt, clenched fists, he wept, "Claire, why does she make me so angry?!" I had no answer, I could only commiserate. My older brother Christopher, aged ten, accidentally put a garden fork through his wellington boot. He spent a day walking over fields, ditches, and barbed wire fences to bury the evidence, but every time he thought he had found the perfect place, the terror overwhelmed him, he knew she would find it and he would be punished. Only at nightfall was he able to leave it under a bush and make the long trek home. It was rare that our shared experience of mother could be voiced. To this day, even after her passing, our private conversations feel disloyal, we find ourselves looking over our shoulders, still in the experience of her paranoia, and ours.

# CHAPTER NINETEEN

B ack in the school office, Arthur, the oldest and longest-serving member of the department, was so overburdened and disgruntled that his wife, a dead ringer for Popeye's wife Olive, spent nearly every school day, and some days in the holidays too, in the cupboard at the back of his classroom working for no money.

"That is going to stop," said Alexandra, "Cynthia will have to be paid for all the work she does."

Arthur muttered under his breath, "Like that's ever going to happen. She has no idea."

But it *did* happen. Everything Alexandra said she would make happen did indeed happen, even though her steamroller approach caused upset on more than one occasion. "It's about the kids," she said, "we have to make it happen for the kids, they only get one shot at school and we are it."

Walking back to my car, on her first day, I could barely speak. Malcolm, the deputy headmaster, asked me, "So Claire, oops I mean Fiona, what did you think of the new boss?"

I coughed as though I needed to clear my throat, but I was actually masking emotion. I mumbled a matter of fact, "She seems great," and then weakly repeated, "Yes great." I was attempting to hide the explosion going on in my head and heart. She had come in like the cavalry, awakening a sense of purpose and dedication to my vocation as a teacher.

More than that, in the time it took to feel the warmth of her handshake and the depth of feeling in her dark brown eyes, I felt as if I loved her.

Thank God she was married. I was safe.

I spent more and more time in Alexandra's office. My physical and mental strength were returning. We devoted hours of our time to plans and schemes for making lessons more interesting. A change in the law now prevented students from giving up a language at fourteen and, consequently, we were stuck with a pack of fifteen-year-olds enraged that they had to continue to learn French. Alexandra's solution was to take the entire year group to France. The school would have to subsidise the trip; these kids were demotivated and disenfranchised across all their subjects.

"You can't take David Solomon," said every one of his teachers, "he will be a liability. In fact, the last trip he went on ended up at the police station."

"That's exactly why he has to go," said Alexandra, "he needs it more than anyone."

Some teachers refused to accompany the group when they saw the list of miscreants.

"That's fine," said Alexandra, "I only want staff who understand what I'm doing."

Thomas, the hippy in the department who had given up taking trips many years before, warned her, "With the changes in the law, you have to protect yourself. Parents will sue at the drop of a hat. The legalities and insurance now are out of control. We are totally exposed if anything goes wrong."

"You're right," she said, "and to me, it's worth the risk. What else are we doing this for, if we don't manage to have an impact on the disaffection, we will be paying for it in the classroom all year long."

Thomas, the jaded cynic who had been ostracized by other teachers for his alternative lifestyle and alternative way of teaching was invited into Alexandra's office where she told him how his pupils needed him on that trip, how he reached them in a way that no other teacher did, and she would respect his choice but she wanted him there. I remember his beaming face as he sat at the front of the bus as we headed out to Calais, his pride in his chosen profession restored. Alexandra did that to all of us, and it wasn't long before the kids' results started to climb and we were being cited as a centre for excellence and good practice.

Eventually, after months of working late at close quarters, talking only about work, I plucked up the courage to ask Alexandra for a conversation of a more personal nature. Finding my voice had become the theme of my recovery throughout my illness and now I had to speak up. I could tolerate being kept at arms' length no longer. I had proven myself to be competent and reliable. I hadn't missed a day of work. I was getting stronger, I was energised. My delight, seeing her each morning at work seemed to be reciprocated. I had made myself utterly available for every improvement scheme that she instigated and I felt as if I had earned a more personal connection.

Huddled in that gloomy office at the end of a long day, my heart pounding, I spoke the unspeakable, "Alexandra, do you think we could ever talk about stuff other than work? Do you ever think about us being friends outside of work? It feels as if we are already friends, and maybe you just want to keep it professional, but sometimes I think of us doing other stuff together, talking about things outside

*Fiona Goodwin*

work and I feel we have got to know each other really well. I think about meeting your family…" I trailed off. It had come out in a rush.

There was a silence. She stuttered, "Well, I have a big job to do here Fiona, and really every moment counts and then when I go home, my kids have already been on their own for more than a couple of hours. I appreciate what you're saying but it's really a matter of hours in the day." She said the words clearly but slightly forlornly, as if part of her had not signed off on her inner agreement. There was something she wasn't saying. There was a kind of pleading for understanding in her eyes and tone, like "please don't push me, this is all I can do right now."

I was heartened. "Well I understand." My therapist had told me that the outcome of the conversation was less important than my speaking my truth. "I just needed to say it. I hope you don't mind."

"No of course not." Her quick response told me she was happy with her answer but also happy that what had previously been unspoken between us had now been brought out into the open.

To break the tension, I scooped up the dirty cups from the various desks. That's what I did. That was my job. I cleaned up. "I'll just get these done."

"Great, thanks." She didn't look up.

Nothing was ever the same after that. Unbeknownst to me, I heard years later, she had gone home that night and asked for a conversation with her husband. They had been together since college. She sat him down, "I don't know what to do," she told him, "I've told you about the teacher in my department who was sick for a really long time, and that they said would probably go off work again. Well, she's been doing really well. In fact, I couldn't have done all that I'm doing without her. Well, my feelings for her are really strong. I don't understand what they are exactly. I just know that I feel very deeply about her."

Martin had listened with his usual kindness and, without a trace of concern, responded, "Is it a physical thing?"

"Good Lord! No!" The idea was truly horrifying to her.

"Well what's the problem then?" he asked. "She sounds great and you could use a friend, especially with us being new here. I think it would be good for you to be less isolated, to have interests and friends of your own. You know how work can take over."

What she didn't tell him was her reaction to our first meeting. She had noticed the blue of my eyes. She did not lie about there being no physical attraction. It was unconscionable to her. In her mind it did not exist.

# CHAPTER TWENTY

My growing awareness that she maybe had feelings for me but just had no room for me was gratifying. The Bette Davis film "Now Voyager" that I had watched with the Mother Superior in Italy came to mind: "Don't let's ask for the moon. We have the stars." I could never have a relationship with this woman but I could be in her life and she in mine. I found great comfort in that. I resolved not to pressure her and was taken completely by surprise at the end of the week as I replaced the clean cups on the shelf.

"Have you ever seen the rose garden at Kew?" she asked.

I took a deep breath and carried on stacking cups. "No, I haven't. I've heard it's very beautiful." I made that up. It sounded like an invitation was on its way. I tried to sound as relaxed as I could.

"Well I would love to go there," she continued, "and Martin isn't interested and I suppose I wondered if that would go some way to responding to your request of last week?"

Oh my goodness! She was referencing last week's conversation! My heart was in my mouth. I didn't mention how bored I was by gardens or that this was my mother's favourite occupation and that I had been dragged around botanical gardens all over the world and experienced the same unfathomable boredom in all of them! No, I didn't say that because the destination was immaterial. I could easily ignore the presence of the plants and the Japanese water features, "That sounds lovely, when were you thinking?"

"Tomorrow? Why don't you come over to my house and we can go from there?" She carefully adjusted the position of the stapler onto the top right-hand corner of a large collection of papers, then applied just enough pressure with the palm of her hand to hear the click of the staple cleanly bringing them all together.

"Sure," I was still playing it cool, "you'll have to give me an address. What time are you thinking?"

Without looking up, she opened up the stapler and then reached into the cardboard box on her desk, loaded in another row, and closed it up. She grabbed a post-it and scribbled her address, "Come at two. I think they close at five on a Saturday."

It sounded like this plan had been thought through. This was not a spur-of-the-moment thing.

"Lovely, that sounds great." I matched her nonchalance by reaching for my school bag, gently placing it on the table we were sharing, and filling it with the thirty-two, Year Nine exercise books that needed marking. Years of not showing a single feeling on my face was how I disguised the unspeakable joy of that moment. I decided to leave work early, knowing that I would not have to wait all the way till Monday to see her again. I grabbed my tan sheepskin coat from the peg behind the door and slowly put my arms into the sleeves and buttoned in the warmth at the front. I swung the bag of books over my shoulder, grabbed my battered leather briefcase, then, in the doorway, "I'll see you then, then. Have a good evening."

She glanced up and flashed a smile, "You too. Thanks for your help tonight."

"Not at all."

Tomorrow it would be just me and her, and a few roses. Walking to my blue Volkswagen Golf, I was aware of not having taken a breath for a very long time. I fumbled in the front pocket of the briefcase for my keys, opened the door, and swung the bags over the gear stick onto the passenger seat. I sat, holding the wheel, staring out in front of me. As was often the case, the only cars remaining in the car park were mine, Alexandra's, and the caretaker's. It was ten to six. The sports teams had been and gone. I pushed away the thought of Alexandra's three teenagers waiting to be fed at home.

I slept only sporadically that night.

"We are simply going to see a garden, it's just a garden, it's just for a few hours, it's not a big deal!" I argued back and forth.

I woke up at two in the morning, and unable to sleep, I went downstairs to make a cup of tea. The neat pile of unmarked books waited on the dining room table. The blue of the covers matched the blue of the sofa, the blue of the carpet, and the flecks in the otherwise yellow bespoke roman blinds. Everything was yellow or blue or yellow and blue. Even the chunky hand-made pottery teapot had a deep blue glaze. I poured the tea into the matching mug.

"This is a very big deal, she is very busy, she has a husband and children and she is choosing to take time out from them, from her routine, to spend time with me."

I put the teapot and mug on a tray with a jug of milk. It was going to be a long night. I calmed myself with the thought, "She loves gardens and just needs someone to go with her, it could be anyone. Her husband is most probably like me and can't stand gardens."

Back in my bedroom, I lay the tray on the bed and gingerly climbed under the covers, anxious not to spill it everywhere.

No, it couldn't be just anyone because when she invited me she didn't make eye contact, she played around with the stapler. It was too big a deal for her. Normally she would be openly enthusiastic. She was playing it down, like me.

I eventually resorted to flicking on the television to a prerecorded episode of Moonlighting—still my favourite show. The sexual tension between Cybil Shepherd and Bruce Willis was a welcome distraction. What an unlikely couple and yet how inevitable the outcome.

For breakfast, I ate whole wheat brown toast with butter and ginger marmalade. I was hungry, it had been a long night. I ground the coffee beans and poured the potent dark roast from the silver cafetière. The aroma was familiar and comforting and continental. I watched the clock. She was always late but I mustn't be. I drank the coffee and didn't put the radio on. I washed up and put everything away before reaching for my coat and keys. I was wearing newly washed blue jeans and a Benetton sweater, scruffy cowboy boots, and a brown leather knee-length coat. She had only ever seen me in work clothes. I told myself that this was nothing, knowing that this was not nothing. My heart was pounding and I was on a ride that I would not get off for over eleven years. I didn't know that then. I wonder if I had known, would I have done anything different that day? I don't think so.

*Fiona Goodwin*

# CHAPTER TWENTY-ONE

On the morning of the rose garden, I left in plenty of time and pottered up the Hampstead High Road. A grand two-storey Edwardian corner house with huge beech trees in the garden. Behind the wooden gates the drive was littered with bikes, a carpentry bench, and bats and rackets of all sorts: cricket, croquet, badminton. I left the car on the street and walked up the steps to a grand double fronted doorway. The bell loudly announced my arrival and I heard a distant, "Coming!!!" She was running down the stairs and then footsteps across a stone floor. The right-hand door with a stained glass window and large brass knob swung back.

Her face was triumphant and flustered: black jeans and sweater and short black riding boots. Her hair and wide eyes looked darker and more striking. Her arms were full of children's clothes, "The kids are still in bed and Martin's gone to a car rally. Let me put these in the machine and then I'll grab my coat before someone wants something! How was the journey? You found it all right from your place?"

She was talking politely, in her professional voice. I replied in a similar vein, "The journey was very good, thank you, Mrs. Carlton. Your instructions were excellent." She caught the sarcasm and blushed slightly, "Oh it's going to be like that is it?" She smiled.

"Well yes, if you're going to talk to me in your teacher voice!"

"I see!" With her eyebrows raised, she smiled, but I could see she was slightly disconcerted by my impertinence, "In that case, get in the bloody car Goodwin!"

"That's better!"

I was so impressed and a little shocked by my handling of my boss who, at work, was always so large and in charge. Well, we were no longer on her territory. She was not my boss here and I felt that I detected some relief in her response to my reprimand. We got in the car, a tiny white Fiesta and she seemed happy to be in the driving seat.

"Wow this is great!" she gushed, "a few hours of doing no work, no washing, and no whining! I don't really care where we go except that the botanical gardens are right near where I grew up and I would love to show you my old house." She chattered on, "I don't remember when I last climbed over the wall and made a bid for freedom!"

I could feel her excitement and delight. Good, I thought, I'm helping her get much-needed time out." I felt useful. The fact that she wanted to show me her childhood home took me unawares. She had never previously mentioned her childhood or anything remotely personal and here we were going right to the heart of the matter.

"Yes," she said, "my father was an industrialist, and an alcoholic and my mother was schizophrenic. She got sick, he started drinking and eventually pretty much lost the business. It was so chaotic. I used to be chauffeur-driven to school in a black Bentley wearing my brother's underpants back to front. My brother was the son and heir and was given everything and I was the daughter and though I was sent to an expensive public school, my mother was frugal, she preferred not to have to spend money on buying me separate underwear. I would dread the end of the day, wondering if Father was going to pick me up. It was terrifying. I lay in the drive one time trying to stop him going out in the car drunk. We lost God knows how many luxury cars to the gatepost or the ditch outside the house."

It poured out of her. I listened. We forgot we were colleagues as we went through the entrance of the botanical gardens. I sensed that the flowers were not going to be intruding on our time together. In the chilly spring air, we wandered over the lawns and through rhododendrons and into the rose garden. Months of professional distance melted. The desire to put my arm through hers was intense. Instead, I stuffed my hands firmly in my pockets and as if a dam had broken, we ramblingly confided our stories. Our life together began that day in the rose garden.

The botanical gardens were everything they were meant to be. The perfume of the roses was intoxicating. I was a convert. The reds and flaming oranges and lemony yellows, the colours more vivid as the morning progressed and the comfort and contentment in each other's voices, more exquisite. There was a tearoom where we sat outside on the patio on white wrought iron chairs, preferring to be in chilly sunshine than inside surrounded by people. We sipped the steaming Earl Grey tea from china cups and shared a wedge of chocolate cake.

"We're going to France for Easter", she said it slowly as if knowing its impact. I felt it viscerally in my solar plexus.

"We're staying at the cottage," she continued, "you know I've told you about our place down near Aix en Provence?"

"Yes", I nodded slowly. I was catapulted out of the reverie of tea and cake and sunshine back into the reality of her and me. The rug had been pulled, we were work colleagues, and she had a life apart from me.

"We leave on Saturday, you could come for lunch before we go if you like?"

I had been giddy with tea and roses and then there was the feeling of being pushed off a cliff and now I was being rescued with an invitation to meet the family. What a rollercoaster!

"I would like that, thank you."

"Good," she said. "We should get going now. We promised Max we would go to the rescue shelter this afternoon and look for a dog for him."

Saturday came. The intervening days at school had been a little awkward, she was back to being the boss, professionalism paramount, but there was a knowing, a relief.

On arrival at her house, their people carrier stood in the drive loaded with bikes on the back and bags on the roof.

"Max, bring your bag down" I heard a man shout, "I need it now!"

I wandered up to the back door, Alexandra saw me through the kitchen window, "Woohoo! Come on in!" I opened a beaten-up wooden door and stepped onto the Minton mosaic floor.

"Come into the kitchen!" the sound of her voice, so inviting. I made my way from what would have been the scullery, through a wide paneled door to a high ceilinged hallway. Again, the windows were stained glass, complementing the strikingly colourful tiled floor. It felt grand and lived in and welcoming. The kitchen door swung open onto a polished wooden floor and behind Alexandra's bright delighted face, I saw the light pouring in from French windows and a conservatory. The only sign of lunch was an unopened pack of mincemeat by the cooker.

"Leaving in half an hour, everybody!" a frustrated man's voice.

"He likes to leave in plenty of time," smiled Alexandra, "and it's never going to happen," and then loudly, "Martin, come and meet Fiona."

The door swung back and the frustrated voice became a warm laughing face,

"Hi Fiona! Heard so much about you, lovely to meet you finally!" He was broad, medium height, dark wavy hair, brushed cotton checked shirt tucked into brown corduroys. He continued cheerily, "Staying for lunch I hope?" Big enthusiastic smile.

"Thank you, yes, lovely to meet you."

He reached out his hand and clasped mine warmly. The door behind him smashed open against the wall as a lanky teenage girl whizzed into the kitchen, long auburn hair flying, traversing the polished wooden floor at high speed, on rollerblades. Same cheerful face.

"Hiya!" She crashed to a breathless halt against the French dresser, setting the decorative crockery rattling. "Oops!" She grabbed a pine-backed chair to balance as she pulled off the boots. Without looking up from cleaning the sink, Alexandra asked, "Cassie could you get the mince on?"

From the hallway came another girl's voice, "Mum I'll do it, Cassie hasn't packed yet."

In came Melissa, the not-so-tall eighteen-year-old with a long dark plait down her back and again a big smile. "Hi there!"

As she put out her hand, Alexandra explained, "Melissa, this is Fiona, a colleague from work. Fiona, this is Melissa, my eldest." Melissa carried on to the stove, "Mum, are you ready to go?"

Alexandra was now opening a jar of olives and pouring them into a ramekin. She handed it to me, "Olive, Fiona? Lunch won't be long."

Melissa repeated more insistently, "Mum, have you packed?"

"Yes, darling. Just a few things I need to find."

Melissa raised her eyebrows, "Just a few? Can you go and do that now while I do the lunch?"

"No, darling. That would be rude, we have a visitor. I'll do it in a minute. I promise I'm almost there."

"If you're sure..." Melissa was now chopping an onion and pouring olive oil in a pan. Her tone was disbelieving.

As Alexandra was throwing things from the fridge into a cool box, she shouted, "Has anyone seen Max?"

"He's playing football in the garden," Melissa was quick to respond, "He says he's packed but he seems to only have a pair of shorts and swimming trunks."

"Well that's probably all he'll need" Alexandra replied. She banged on the window, "Martin, can you check on Max, I think he's in the garden." Then she turned to me, "Sorry Fiona, it's a bit chaotic, have another olive." She pushed them towards me with hands still covered in soapsuds as she was now cleaning the fridge. "It will all calm down in a minute."

Realising there was now only twenty minutes till departure, I tried, "Is there anything I can do to help?"

"Absolutely Fiona," Martin said, now back in the kitchen grabbing wine glasses, "You can help us drink this up." He placed a half-finished bottle on the table, "Shame to waste it!" he smiled, then shouted out of the back door, "Max, have I got to get your bag or are you going to bring it?"

Then louder, "Max!" and to himself, "Those bloomin' head-phones!" Finally, he got Max's attention just as the football narrowly missed the glass of the conservatory.

"Sorry, Dad! I didn't hear you!"

"Max, I've told you not to kick it this way!"

"Sorry, Dad!"

"Go and get your bag, boy." Under her breath, Melissa muttered, "There's no point him bringing his bag Dad, there's nothing in it!"

"Well, he doesn't need much Melissa, as long as he has his Walkman and a pack of cards he'll be fine."

I sat at the long antique pine table and sipped my wine. From across the cavernous hallway. I heard a slightly hal-tering rendition of one of Brahms's piano concertos, some-one, presumably Cassie, was now playing the piano. The pasta was bubbling away on the stove and the rich smell of Bolognese sauce brought Martin and Max into the kitchen. "Hmm, smells great Mel," he dipped his finger into the boil-ing sauce and stuck it in his mouth. Melissa didn't react, kept stirring.

Alexandra introduced us "Max, did you meet Fiona?"

"Oh no! Hi Fiona!" He was about eleven and charming with blond shoulder-length hair and a fringe hanging over his eyes, grasping my hand, "Are you staying for lunch?"

He possessed the same warmth as his father.

"Yes, thanks Max, I am."

As if to reassure me, he said, " Mel makes a *wicked* spag bog, don't you Mel!?"

"Thanks, Max," she replied and followed it up with a loud, "Cassie!"

"Coming!" came from Cassie as the piano lid slammed shut and soon everyone was seated around the table. Alexandra served the spaghetti and Melissa poured on the sauce. Garlic bread that I hadn't even noticed go in the oven, was tossed onto a breadboard in the middle of the table and everyone dived in, ripping off chunks.

"Well Fiona, you have caught us at our best," said Martin laughing. And I had, I felt that. They were at their best. I felt myself fall in love with each one of them that day. Their collective excitement about setting off for France was contagious. I wanted to go with them. I felt deflated as the table was cleared and the final items thrown in the back of the car and they disappeared down the road waving goodbye. There was a lump in my throat and Alexandra's breezy good-bye felt forced. There was no mistaking the pain of separation.

There was something so endearing about that lunch invitation an hour before they were supposed to leave the country. No one batted an eyelid. The entire family, so generous and embracing.

# CHAPTER TWENTY-TWO

'm not sure how I occupied myself that Easter holiday. I must have done something but it has no place in my memory. I just remember waiting, counting the days till they returned. My life on hold, just the way as a schoolgirl, day after day on cold winter's nights, I used to stand outside the school gate, often missing the regular bus just to get a glimpse of Catherine, Rosie, Jennifer, and on and on....

"Claire what are you still doing here?" they would ask.

"Oh, I had to help Miss Leatherhead with her display" or "rehearsing for the play" or "chess club" or "hockey match." With greater confidence, that morphed into an ironic, "Waiting for you of course!" and they would fall about laughing. I disguised my true intentions with ever-growing comedic flare. It was also true that I didn't particularly want to go home, but mostly, the more time I spent at school, the more chance I had of running into one of them. Even a glimpse, or if I was lucky, a brief conversation, eased the heartache. I had perfected the art of stalking, which led me, often, to tortured thoughts of demonic possession, "I'm sick, I'm no different from a pedophile."

Now at age thirty-four, I was still tortured. On the first day back at school after the Easter Break, I played it cool with Alexandra, just offering a breezy, "Hello boss! How was your holiday?" I barely waited for the answer, it was all so chaotic in the mornings and I sped off to my classroom. For the most part, that day, I stayed away from the office.

I was packing my bag to leave for the day when she called from the office, "Hey Goodwin, come for dinner! Everyone would love to see you! Melissa's cooking, I'm just phoning in the recipe."

I thought I would die of happiness. I sauntered into her office where she was hurriedly shoving papers into a box with the phone tucked under her chin. "No darling, use the courgettes we brought back from France and put a bottle of Puys Fuissé in the fridge, you know, out of the case in the pantry, oh and there's one extra, Fiona's coming for dinner." She looked up and smiled. Her not having actually waited for my response to the invitation felt like a warm blanket being thrown around me. I breathed in the sense of inclusion. She continued, "There's some endive and Roquefort that need to go on the table and just lightly sauté the chicken thighs, then take the skin off before you add the stock and then add the courgette." She paused, "No, don't use the paste darling, there's fresh garlic in the boot of the car from the Bonnaire's garden." She looked over at me, smiling and shaking her head in horror. "Is Daddy home yet? Ok, well can you phone him and if it's not too late tell him to pick up some bread and milk on the way? Is Max back? What's he doing?" the question sounded anxious, "Oh bloody hell, how high has he climbed? Oh God, tell him not to go above the first floor. Dad said the bricks on the side of the house are loose and he should be wearing a helmet." She listened again, "I'm leaving now...no really I am...home in half an hour, thank you, darling, love you!" Then to me, "How clever's that! Having such a brilliant daughter! She practically runs the place!" Her adoration and admiration for her daughter was unbridled. "She is quite amazing, she's doing five A levels, a bit of a clever clogs," and grabbing her briefcase and a heavy plastic box of folders, "Let's go! Do you want to follow me? I know the quick way home."

I nodded, "Sure, let me help you with that." I grabbed the other end of the box and we struggled out through the doors together.

Dinner was as delightful and as chaotic as the previous time. It was as if we were celebrating. In fact, there was champagne to start with, the rationale for that was explained, "First day back at school is sooo painful, we always try to take the edge off it. In France we forget all about work and then wham, back in harness for another six weeks." She tipped the glass back, "Drink up!"

The feast had been prepared and Cassie was called to lay the table. Max was hanging from a window ledge on the second floor. "He'll be fine, he can't hurt himself," Martin reassured Alexandra, "I'm going to make that side of the house into a climbing wall. It's perfect for technique and strength-building. He'll either fall into the hedge or onto grass."

"He's not wearing a helmet," Alexandra protested, "just get him in for dinner please, it's ready."

"Max!" Martin shouted out of the back door. "Dinner's on the table." From way up high, there was a faint, "Coming!" and then an almighty thud, as he presumably dropped from a great height.

"This house is sooo cool!" Max declared, out of breath, lowering himself onto the dining room chair, feet off the ground, one hand on the back of the chair and one hand on the table.

"Wash your hands Max, please, you've been touching dirty bricks."

"Ah, ok mum! For you!" he smiled his cheeky smile, "Hi Fiona, how was your holiday? Ours was fantastic!" He stood up and waited for my answer.

"Great. Thanks, Max."

"Excellent!"

"Max! Hands!"

"Sure Dad, I'm on it." He good-naturedly left the room, whistling through his teeth and there was the sound of running water and he came back into the kitchen and flicked water from his wet hands at Cassie, "Watcha Cassie!" She protested, "Max! Stop it!'

"Puy Fuissé anyone?!' Martin beamed as he popped the cork, "Happy first day back everyone!"

Once poured, the glasses were clinked together,

"Cheers everyone! Welcome, Fiona! And it's our last day without a dog! Getting him from the kennels tomorrow!' There was a big cheer.

"Remember what I told you," Martin was addressing everyone, "I'm not doing all the walking."

"Yes you are!" chorused Alexandra and the children.

"Dad you *know* you will be doing all the walking!" That was Cassie.

"That's not what we agreed." He sounded adamant.

"Too late now Dad, you've paid for him!" Martin smiled, "Oh well, see what I have to put up with Fiona!"

I didn't want to leave that house, not that night, not ever. The dinner cleared away, Alexandra and I sat in the conservatory into the night, drinking red wine and talking endlessly about school and dogs and France and the children.

"You'll have to come with us next time! You know, at the last minute when we were leaving I was so close to tell-

*Fiona Goodwin*

ing you just to jump in the car! If there had been room, I probably would have!"

I was bowled over, hearing her say what I had sensed. I had been right, she hadn't wanted to leave me behind. She rarely showed her hand but when she did, oh my, the warmth of her affection was undeniable.

Nothing was the same after that night—we became a fixture most evenings in the chilly conservatory. Martin found an electric heater for us. We wore thick sweaters and when the piles of books were marked and lessons prepared, we talked endlessly, later and later into the night. I often spent nights on the couch in the study. The sleeping bag became sheets and a duvet, and the sheets and duvet eventually became a bed in the spare room. I dreaded going back to my own home on weekends, so sometimes I wouldn't. Couldn't. The flurry and joy of being with the family was too intoxicating. The loss of the church community had left a void and the Carltons had adopted me. I felt like I belonged for the first time. The English summer days were getting warmer and one Friday Alexandra announced, "This weekend I'm going to paint your toenails red."

That night, I confided in my analyst. He rarely spoke or changed his expression but when I told him about the nail-painting, his left eyebrow flickered slightly. I sensed his concern. I have to find a man I decided. On my return home, I signed up for, "Tea for Two," a heterosexual matchmaking service. I told Alexandra at school the next day that I needed to talk. I wanted to let her know that I needed some space, but before I could finish my sentence, she interjected with, "Actually Fiona, I have to talk to you too." She was playing with her pearls, "I think we should have a Victorian evening."

"I'm sorry? A what?!"

"A Victorian evening! It's a sleepover! Just us."

I was stunned. "Ah," was all I could say.

"And what were you wanting to say to me?" She waited for my answer. My resolve to find a man had instantly dissolved, "Nothing really, it's gone out of my head."

The following Friday, as she grabbed her briefcase to leave work, she announced, "All the family are gone this weekend. Tomorrow night is the Victorian night!" She said it with a flourish as if she were announcing the opening of a long-awaited spectacle.

I arrived that Saturday evening, there was music, low lighting, candles. There were shadows dancing on the walls, "First there's dinner," she said, "boeuf bourguignon!" How Victorian would this night be, I wondered…

We ate heartily and finished off a bottle of Shiraz. I realised I was nervous, this felt so intimate. After the meal, she stood to her feet somewhat formally. She grabbed an article of clothing, it was faded white. She spoke like a priest offering the sacrament, "This is your Victorian nightie. Go! Put it on!" The nightie was heavily starched cotton, long-sleeved with an embroidered buttoned-up high ruff neck. As she draped it over my outstretched arms, I studied it. I wondered what it meant. Looking up at her I stepped away and went to the bathroom to change. I was keen to do her bidding. A few minutes later she called from the lounge, "You can come in now!" I emerged from the bathroom, wearing the nightie, feeling like the lady of the manor on her wedding night. Was this a wedding gown or was it merely something to sleep in? With each step I cared less, pushing away the flashes of fear, the path to damnation. I tentatively pushed open the door of the lounge and caught the soft sound of Edith Piaf singing, "Non, je ne regrette rien." It was dark but from the flickering light of the candles, I made out her face crinkled up in a smile. She was wearing an identical full-length nightie. Giggling, she held out one of the two glasses of champagne that she was holding. A double mattress was lying shamelessly in front of the flaming log fire, presumably she had dragged it downstairs. No mean feat. I grinned back at her, our eyes locked, I took the glass that she was offering and studied the scene she had created. Again my mind and body were asking what exactly did this mean? I had walked onto a movie set where the script had yet to be written. My heart was telling me what I wanted, and what I was too scared to want. We sat down on the mattress, cross-legged, biting into ripe strawberries from a silver platter. We raised our glasses and she smiled a toast, "To the Victorians!" We shrieked with laughter and took big gulps of champagne. We were transported. We were the Brontë's, innocence itself. We lay down and collapsed again into laughter because the hundred-year-old nighties kept ripping. I was praying, God give me strength! I just wanted to throw my arms around her, but instead, we just lay there, close, all night. When she turned towards the fire, I snuggled up behind her and we slept. I thought of Andrea, the heat of the jungle, the longing and the impossibility.

The next morning, the nighties were in shreds but I was relieved (mostly but not entirely) that nothing had happened. Our Brontë sister status was intact. We returned the mattress to the spare room and went to the kitchen for breakfast. The air between us was thick. I was still in a state of yearning. I was leaning against the kitchen wall, waiting for the kettle to boil when she came up to me and without any warning, kissed me on the lips.

"What was that?" I stuttered.

"Nothing."

"That wasn't nothing. I'm not sure that that was a very good idea."

"Why not?"

"This is why not," and without thinking, I took her face in my hands and I kissed her back. After months of concealing my feelings, I finally really kissed her. She didn't immediately pull back. When she did, all the colour drained from her face. She left the room. No explanation. The next thing I heard was the roar of the vacuum cleaner being wrenched back and forth across the lounge carpet where we had slept. Clearing away the evidence of unfulfilled longing. The awkwardness was like cold water being poured over the joy of that night. Nothing more was said about the kiss.

Unrequited love, all too familiar to me, took me to my practical self. I had to find my balance, get back on the *straight* and narrow. After a few days of pining and calling myself an idiot, I did what any good, closeted lesbian would do, I decided to go back to men.

That's what led me to Bob.

# CHAPTER TWENTY-THREE

remember driving to our first blind date—we met on Tea for Two. He was standing outside the restaurant, round and short and bald, like an English Danny DeVito. I just kept driving. Then I thought "No Fiona, you can't do that to the man. You're not even a real woman, and Danny DeVito is adorable." So I turned around and drove back again.

I went out with this man for a while. He had a great big motorbike, one of those zero to sixty in four seconds, a Ducati I think. Two weeks into our relationship, he had been taking me out for lovely expensive dinners, we hadn't yet had sex, in fact, I was thirty-eight and technically still a virgin but I was determined to have heterosexual sex, even if it killed me. That's when Bob said, "Darling, would you like to go away for a night?"

"Oh God this is it!" I felt sick to my stomach. It reminded me of taking cod liver oil as a child—it was something extremely distasteful that just had to be done.

He picked me up in his Jaguar. It was the XK8 Sovereign, metallic mint green, a stunning car. An upgrade on the basic XJ6. I knew they had had problems with oil leaks but I didn't mention it, I thought it would be a dead giveaway, lesbian-wise. He was wearing orange elasticated baggy shorts and a large white t-shirt with a picture of Windsor Safari Wildlife Park—elephants and rhinoceroses and a giraffe on the front. The worst thing was, he had awful B.O. I thought "No Fiona, brace up, you have to do this!" He was kind, keen on me, and rich. I might be unhappy but I knew I would be well taken care of.

After a couple of hours driving, we turned into a tiny airport, "Where are we going?" I was anxious.

"Alderney," he said.

"On a plane?"

"Yah, it's literally just off the coast before you get to France."

I looked at the tickets. He had booked us for four nights. I had specifically said one.

"Oh don't worry about that darling, we can fly you back anytime." But a tiny woman behind a tiny desk said, "Actually Alderney is currently fog bound. Nothing's landing or taking off at the moment."

That's when I learned that Alderney was part of the Channel Islands, it's where rich people hide their money. And presumably their lesbian girlfriends. Suddenly it was as if I were in Casa Blanca on the tarmac with Danny DeVito!

We spent the afternoon driving around in a golf buggy, eating lobster. It was three square miles of the most boring place I had ever been to. Bob pointed to a deserted fort, way out on the sand, "Darling, would you like to live there?" I desperately looked for an out, "Well when the tide comes in, it's completely cut off."

"That's not a problem," he was delighted with his solution, "We could get you a helicopter, you would love that." A helicopter? I did like helicopters. And if I had to be with a man—a helicopter might offset that, and I could say that I was going shopping in France but really land in Alexandra's garden. It was a lovely offer. I said I would think about it.

We had a rough night. Neither of us really knew what we were doing. He was slippery from his sweat, like a big slippery mountain. I kept sliding off. I couldn't wait for it to be over. When the snoring starting, I crept out. I was missing Alexandra dreadfully. So I whispered into the hotel phone in the other room. I told her about Bob. She asked, "Do you have your own room?"

"No, we're sharing."

"What??" She went nuts, screaming and sobbing down the phone, quietly, so that her husband wouldn't hear. I felt dreadful. And so confused.

The next morning, I made up a story. I told Bob I had to leave. I took the golf buggy back to the tiny airport. The gentleman in front of me had purchased the last two tickets—one for him and one for his dog. I was desperate, "Sir, I have an awful family emergency. Is there any chance I could have your dog on my lap and I will pay for his ticket?" He was delighted and so, after my night of being squashed by Bob, I spent the next forty-five minutes being squashed by a full-size Labrador called Trevor.

Back in London, I unpacked and opened the mail, there was a card from Alexandra postmarked prior to my weekend with Bob:

*"Darling, all will be well. Martin and the children are leaving for San Moritz early, so you and I can join them later. We'll take the scenic route, and camp on the way."*

My stomach flipped. We barely made it through the Victorian evening. How would we make it through two nights in a tent?

As it happens, we didn't.

The anticipation on the day of our first outing to the rose garden had been intense, but it paled into insignificance compared to this brazen August morning as we threw our bags into the boot. A cooler containing Kitkats, cheese and pickle sandwiches, a whole chicken, and milk for our tea, sat on the backseat. I kept the salt and vinegar crisps and Garibaldi biscuits in a Marks & Spencer's plastic bag at my feet. We were particularly excited about some leftover home-made bread and butter pudding wrapped in foil, and there was a hot flask of Earl Grey tea. We chatted about who would drive first and who would navigate—we wanted to be well into France by nightfall. Naturally, I had very mixed feelings about arriving in St Moritz at all! I took the first shift being in charge of the big road map. It was tempting to choose an even more "scenic" route. I resisted. Watching the road ahead I mused on what was about to happen. I thought about our kiss—there had only ever been one, and here we were, soon to be barrelling down the auto route towards Switzerland. Any sense of Swiss neutrality was rapidly disappearing in the rear-view mirror. I tried not to think about consequences, or the implications for the family. I absolved myself of any responsibility with the notion that if, and only if she made a move, would I respond. It would be rude not to?

At Nordausques in France, at around 7p.m. we came off the autoroute. We found a grassy patch by the river and pitched the tent. Exhausted, we sat in our sleeping bags and munched on the last of the bread-and-butter pudding. We didn't clean our teeth or do any of the normal things. Through the thin wall of our purple dome tent the moonlight cheekily lit up our faces. The mysterious light felt like being in chapel. Thoughts of hell did not belong here, there was too much love. We lay in silence listening to the sounds of the river running close by. Months and months of restraint were swept away in its current as she leaned over and gently placed her lips on mine. I didn't want that night to be over, ever.

The following morning as we held each other's gaze, we knew that this page could never be turned back. We were swimming in heavenly terror.

When we finally reached the family in San Moritz, Alexandra was visibly disoriented.

"Mum," asked Cassie, "you look awful, are you okay?"

"I'm fine darling, I think I must have eaten something that didn't agree with me on the journey."

That was the beginning of our eleven-year secret love affair.

# CHAPTER TWENTY-FOUR

On our return to England, we fell into a regular pattern of her coming to my house one evening a week and there began the real tug of war between us and the family. It was a balancing act of epic proportions.

When, the following year, we were all back in Aix, the rest of the family had their own plans so Alexandra and I set off on our first extended trip together. We headed for Monaco, leaving Aix at 2 p.m., way too late to have a chance of arriving before nightfall, so silly. We were just messing around enjoying the sunny morning. Martin and Max had left for Switzerland typically early, five in the morning. Fishing rods and emergency rations all packed into the van the night before, they were going to be installed on the banks of the Loire for five days. They were gone and I could breathe. For that, I felt ashamed, loving them but loving when they left, felt despicable. Worst of all, Martin was grateful that Alexandra had her best friend while he was gone. His misplaced trust in me felt like a spiritual cancer. I was a pariah. Whenever they left, Alexandra would become pensive, she would rummage, get busy, processing her transition from wife and mother to lover. Her struggle was more complex than mine and, however patient I tried to be, those moments for me were always anxious, lonely ones.

Then, that morning, after three or four hours of awkward silence, she suggested we have a boiled egg with a chunk of baguette and butter—it was a ritual that we had as a family, but normally Martin cooked the eggs. He would stand at the stove of the tumbledown gite, with his high-tech waterproof, bombproof watch and time my egg for three minutes and Alexandra's and the children's for four. We weren't to speak to him when he was timing. It irritated me, the gravitas, the inability to converse and time eggs simultaneously, but now I remember with deep nostalgia his kindness and concentration, not to mention the delight and triumph on his face every time he saw me open a perfectly cooked egg. Alexandra was more cavalier in her egg timing—mostly accurate but more from intuition than design. Her saying, "Let's have a boiled egg," that morning was the sign that she was on her way back to being fully present, we would soon be out of no man's land. The steaming cafetière on the rough surface of the farmhouse table took us the rest of the way. We both reached to steady my mug as she poured and her hand went over mine, we were stopped in our tracks. She looked up. There was no one else there. The coffee smelt so good. Her eyes were mischievous and teasing,

"Cheer up Goodwin!" she laughed. We were home free, through the wall and into the secret garden. We chatted like the long-lost lovers that we were, lost and in love now for 8 years, we were about to set off on one of our "cultural experiences"—that was how we justified our expeditions. I had driven down to Aix to join her and the family in my bright blue convertible—a Fiat Barchetta recently delivered to the UK from Turin. On the rack at the back was strapped an antique green leather trunk with my initials painted in gold, that was where our little purple tent was packed along with the latest technology in sleeping mats, they inflated themselves, they were Martin's idea, and brilliant. Alexandra had bought a matching outfit for the car, everything was blue and we stopped talking every few moments now just to laugh, to clutch our sides and laugh; we were still laughing as we crossed the Italian border four hours later. The border guards laughed with us.

"If only they knew," we kept saying as we tapped our fingers along to Huey Lewis and the News and Django Rhinehart and Nina Simone and Stefan Grapelli—what amazing travel companions they were. It was dark driving into Monaco and it seemed dull, the idea of leaving our blue cocoon, so we just kept driving and the further south we went, the warmer it got. The roof was still down at 3 a.m. as we rolled onto the Ponte Vecchio in Florence. I wasn't sure if it was permitted to drive over it but we were living a morality all of our own and it didn't seem wrong to stop the car in the middle of the bridge. We got out and leaned over the parapet peering into the dark waters of the Arno. We straightened up and gazed at the ancient roofs and twinkling lights and I felt her hand in mine,

"Thank you for bringing me here," she whispered, her eyes glistening. I wiped her tear away with my blue scarf and we put our arms around each other, holding on for dear life like children transported to a magical land. I tried to put out of my mind the impermanence of the moment and just breathe in the warm night. I tried not to think about what would happen in eight days when we would drive back to Aix; I tried just to smell her hair and feel the roughness of her black wool coat and the softness of her cheek against mine. I can still smell and feel all of it. What I know is that I can never go back to Florence. I can never go back to Venice or Malta or Thessalonica or Athens or Rome or Barcelona or Nerja and certainly not to the palace at Alhambra. Most of all I can never go back to Aix…

I dreaded always the cloud that descended on the journey home. She wasn't mine and I knew it. That felt unbearable but what didn't feel unbearable was being a woman with a woman—her soft skin against mine, the smell of her hair, the warmth of her breath, waking up each morning to find ourselves still entwined. It was baffling to me, how something I'd been told was so wrong could feel so right. I never stopped loving her but I spent many a maudlin night trying to see a future for myself. I envisaged ending my days alone in the room next to them in the old folks' home. Our routine continued: Friday nights she stayed later and later at my house and my misery meant that I had begun to sulk at the start of our time together in anticipation of her returning to her house. One of these evenings, Alexandra came through the door, took one look at my face, and sat me down. She held my hands in hers, "Fiona, if this makes you unhappy then it has to stop. I'm not leaving my husband and children. You need to decide. I promise I won't get in the way of your finding someone of your own but in the meantime, we have each other. That has to be enough." She waited for her words to land, and then added, "Tell me, do you want me to stay or do you want me to go?"

She was sat next to me on the sofa, still in her coat, car keys in hand. I looked at the floor, ashamed. Of course I didn't want her to leave her husband and family, I loved them too. Neither did I want the shame of being an *out* lesbian couple—that was unimaginable. But it was so lonely spending time waiting for her to be available. I hated lying to my ever-diminishing circle of friends. I had more sense of belonging than I had ever had and her family was a part of that. My head hurt just thinking about it. I saw no way through but I couldn't let her go, "I'm sorry, I don't mean to be miserable." I squeezed her hand and forced a faint smile. She leaned over and kissed me, "Let's have a glass of wine."

From then on, I resigned myself to the status quo and learned to hide my dissatisfaction.

"We can make it work," were the words she would comfort me with. She did everything she could to make it tolerable, even giving me my own room in her house where, towards the end, I stayed most weeknights.

Despairing as I was of there ever being a happy outcome to our tryst, a way through eventually emerged. I got a promotion to another school and in desperation, I attended some personal growth seminars. The Californian facilitator filled my mind with thoughts of living a bigger, braver life. I wanted to know more and he pointed me in the direction of the University of Santa Monica. The decision to commute to Los Angeles once a month seemed insane but it was confirmed by unexpected funding and permission for time off work. Leaving my house at 6 a.m. on a Friday morning, I could be sat in class at the University of Santa Monica at 6 p.m. that same evening (2 a.m. UK time). I would be back on the plane at 9 p.m. on Sunday night and back at work in London, Tuesday morning. Every month my mind was expanded, my heart moved by hopefulness and an acceptance of who I was.

No one on the course seemed to care about my sexuality. I met people there who were happy and unafraid to be in a same-sex relationship. On the first night, in front of two hundred and forty strangers, in a flood of tears, I confessed, "I don't know what to do, I'm in love with a married woman and I love her and I love her family and I don't want her to leave them but I can't tell anyone and my life is shrinking and I am lying about who I am and who I love." I rambled on, stopping only to gasp for air and to wipe my eyes. The room was silent, two hundred and forty pairs of eyes on me. Some joined in with my crying and others started laughing. Then I started to laugh and then cry again and that made them laugh even more. It was the first time in ten years, apart from with my therapist, that I had spoken about the life I was leading. It was such an extraordinary relief. It was also the moment when it dawned on me how much I loved to tell stories. My sense of humour had been a lifesaver over years being confined in rooms managing disaffected inner-city children, but this was different, they were adults. Their response was surprising. People came up to me, "Fiona you should write the story! This could be a movie! You should do stand-up comedy!" More fantastical nonsense, Americans are always so positive. Mind you, Alexandra and I had always said our story was a film that could never be made...

My renewed energy and aliveness did not go unnoticed back home. Alexandra was suspicious, had I met someone on the California course? I had. I had met a more accepting version of myself. I noticed the relief, getting on the plane at Heathrow every month, knowing that where I was going, I didn't have to lie; it felt like breathing clean air. In the first year of this California adventure, unbelievably I still felt I had to work towards improving my relationships with men, still vainly hoping and believing that resolving the issues with my mother would open up an attraction to the opposite sex. I put myself through psychosexual therapy for that same reason.

It was a bitter conclusion to reach, it felt like a defeat—trying to be straight was hopeless and living a secret life had finally become intolerable. The intoxicating secrecy of the affair had isolated me. Friendships had been curtailed by my guilt at not being able to share my truth. It was time to say goodbye.

# CHAPTER TWENTY-FIVE

The tree outside the balcony at Alexandra's house had to be chopped down. It was an ancient oak. It meant that we could sit outside on balmy evenings and take in the night sky and the smells of newly mown grass and bonfires, and there we were left alone. That tree sheltered us along with so many others, the woods at the back of the house in the park, dense and dark, the trees in the arboretum at Aix and the shrubs and woods by Lake Como, the purple heather and brush in Thessalonica, the hillside woods where we camped in Tourette Sur Loup and the leafy vines on the Via Bolognese on the way to Fiesole. They hid us, didn't judge us, created oases that made our love possible. The magnificent garden oak was chopped down and there was nowhere to hide.

It was in the Easter holiday of 2004 when I sent the letter. I told my elderly neighbour that I had something to post, and that I couldn't tell him what it was about, but that I needed help getting to the letter box. He put his arm through mine and I leaned on him as I could barely put one foot in front of the other. I was nauseous. My legs were moving but it felt as if they could give way at any moment. I was awash with fear and doubt. Something inside broke that day. Nothing would ever be the same. I didn't cry. I needed all my strength to hold my nerve. Nothing had ever felt so cruel. I spent the next few weeks alone in the apartment, lying on the ancient, dark flagstones with my hot, tear-drenched cheeks soothed by their coolness. The chopped-down oak that had sheltered us, was now screeds of tragic rambling pages. I discovered, as I wrote, the lengths to which I had gone to hide my sexuality. All the tortured paths and rabbit holes that I had been willing to go down! For God's sake the half in, half *out* relationship with Alexandra had suited me! We were as complicit as each other in staying in the closet.

A few days later the phone started ringing, and ringing, and ringing. Message after message, pleading, cajoling, begging me to reconsider. I knew if I saw her that I would cave in. She banged on the door, on the windows, "What are you doing?" she shouted. "You can't do this to us! You have to talk to me!" She was beside herself. She came back three days in a row until finally a message was left on my phone saying that she would have to tell Martin everything because she was losing her mind and that once he knew, there was no going back. That I knew. I had naively hoped that we might one day be friends, that something could be salvaged.

I never saw her again. I never saw any of them again.

I pretend sometimes, when I close my eyes, that if I imagine hard enough the phone will ring and it will be her voice, "Fiona, it's Alexandra. I am at the airport." I'll reply, "Stay there, I am on my way," and I'll set off and I'll see her at Los Angeles Airport Arrivals in the distance, alone, in her long coat, an eccentric hat, surrounded by an odd assortment of bags that had a history and a personality all of their own. I feared the power of my love for her and equally, I feared abandoning all of my discoveries; all the hard-earned ground that I had gained in reclaiming my own voice, breathing new possibilities. She told me that her therapist had asked her,

"Are you sure that this is what you want Alexandra?' Are you sure you want to let her go?" Do those words haunt her still? They haunt me. In my deepest moments of grief, I want to scream them across the Atlantic.

The strength to leave someone when you still love them, when there's no guarantee that you will ever love or be loved again, that strength comes from who knows where. I left Alexandra because I knew it would never be just us.

"La vie sans toi, c'est comme un jour sans lumière, un monde où je n'existe pas." (Life without you, is a day without light, a world where I don't exist.")

I continued the commute to the course in LA, I was called on to share less and less, I think because the room would be reduced to the shambles of a comedy club, but then, eighteen months in, an American actress, Holland Taylor, also on the course, stood up to share, "We haven't heard from Fiona for a while and I would personally like to hear what's going on with her," she paused and added, "and she's funny!" There was a roar of applause as I was forced to my feet.

On the penultimate weekend, I stood up, "I know what I am going to do, I am going to move to Los Angeles, live on a boat in the marina, and do stand-up comedy." The whole room rose to its feet, the cheering was deafening. I returned to the UK that weekend and gave in my resignation. A week later an L.A. friend called, "My friend needs someone to cat sit on his boat for a few months this summer, can you do it?"

Another friend called, "We need a comedian for the U.C.L.A. Annual Cancer Benefit, can you come? It's a paid gig." Another friend contacted me, "Why don't you sign up for a film acting course in Los Angeles, I'm a teacher there, I'll recommend you. That way you will get your visa."

The doors didn't just open, they were flung wide. It was the beginning of my understanding of how the universe works. I heard for the first time the words of Goethe, "At the moment of commitment the entire universe conspires to assist you." This was my new religion. La La Land here I come!

# CHAPTER TWENTY-SIX

he dusty western set of Universal Studios, Hollywood. Old dark slatted wooden cabins on a sunbaked street. A little white train carrying tourists passed the end of the street with the muffled sound of the guide over a loud-speaker giving the names of famous actors and films that were made right where I was standing. I was pinned into a full-length satin red dress, two sizes too small. It hugged my ample figure and my breasts bulged, perfect for the role of the saloon madam. I had to fight to get the dress. It had been booked for a French girl whose scene was being filmed at the same time as ours and since she was late, I blustered my way through, "We're ready to shoot. We'll be done before she needs it." The young man in the costume department, frazzled by the rush of actors claiming their costumes, capitulated, and I ran with it to the back of the saloon and wedged myself in. I had ten minutes before I was due on set. Lipstick and eye shadow slathered on, I felt all woman.

I felt strange in the red dress. The tourists were point-ing at me, taking photos, wondering if I was a movie star perhaps? The crew bustled around with cables and cameras. I was slightly embarrassed at how much I was enjoying their appreciative glances. As I approached the steps to the saloon, there was a girl, a curly brunette twenty-something gazing steadily my way. She was wearing a pink Chanel jacket, leaning nonchalantly over the rail where the imaginary horses were tied,

"You're wearing my dress!" Her wide smile showed her perfect teeth. She looked and sounded like a movie star. Flawless olive skin and green-brown pools of eyes. I quipped, "Well you might have a better chance of getting into it! I'm held together with safety pins!" I turned my back towards her to reveal a gaping bare back and the pins holding it all together a few inches above the waistline.

"Hmm, nice cleavage," she laughed, "front and back!" Her self-assured repartee was unnerving, not to mention how she eyed me so intently. Her French accent made her all the more exotic.

Tony, my director, was calling from inside the shadows of the saloon. I tried to be oh so casual as I picked up the front of the dress and, wearing oversized matching red stilettos, I clunked up the wooden steps. I felt the French girl's eyes on my bare back as I pushed back the doors. For the first scene, there was an angry exchange with a young, drunken cowboy at the bar, which resulted in my tossing whisky in his face. We did close ups and wide shots and I was melting under the lights and thinking about the pink jacketed ingénue outside. The director shouted,

"Ok cut! Everybody outside!"

I clunked back to the sunlight of the saloon doors. I saw pink through the slats and my heart skipped a beat. The brightness blinded me momentarily as I swung both doors outwards, then I clutched the rail and steadied myself down the steps and on to the street. She was exactly where I had left her, a flash of a smile.

In the middle of the street, at the sound of "Action!, I raised the shiny Colt '38. Eyes narrowed, staring into the sun, I pointed the gun at the drunken cowboy and pulled the trigger. He slumped to the ground. I was aware of pink and being watched and the blue of the sky and the whirring camera went silent.

"That's a money shot!" Tony was pleased. "Ok Fiona, you're done, thank you." Being on the lot of Universal Studios, one might assume that Tony was a famous director and that I had landed a part in a Hollywood movie. Not quite. I was enrolled at the New York Film Academy where we had access to the iconic Los Angeles film sets to make short films.

Out of the corner of my eye, I could see pink coming towards me, "You're a piece of work," she grinned, "and now I need to get that dress off you for my scene." My stomach flipped. Was that innuendo? I barely missed a beat, "Easy tiger, I just shot a cowboy." She laughed and pulled out a packet of King size Marlborough slims, "Do you smoke?" I didn't. "Thank you, I'd love one." I took the cigarette from her outstretched hand. She flicked the silver lighter and I dragged on the cigarette, hoping not to choke,

"I'm Fiona,"

She nodded, "And I'm Juliette."

Our half-finished cigarettes were stubbed out in the dirt and we made our way back to wardrobe. I feigned nonchalance as I reappeared in jeans and t-shirt, the dress in hand, "*You* won't be needing the safety pins!"

"No," she said, "I won't. Too bad! That open back was a great look." She winked. She took the dress and, with one final teasing glance, wandered into the gloomy cabin to change.

I decided that however much I wanted to wait for her, not being there when she re-emerged in the dress was the cooler thing to do. I was 46 and I wasn't going to be a hanger on and her flirting with me, I decided, was just her french-ness, and so I reluctantly walked away. The thrill that I felt inside when I was around her did not bode well. As in my teenage days, I felt this could only ever be a fantasy.

At the end of the day, I saw her again with other students sheltering in the shade of a jacaranda tree. I planned to walk past and ignore her, but she called out, "Hey Fi! Hey guys! This is the British shooter from the saloon! She killed a cowboy today!" They laughed as I sauntered over. She introduced me to the others; they were talking about going to the Smoke House.

"Fi, do you want to join us?" That was Juliette. I had a nickname already! I breathed in silently and deeply, my expression impassive and unruffled, "Sure, I'm not doing anything."

Oh my God! The most beautiful girl in the world had just asked me out, not on a date obviously, three other people were coming. I despised myself for the lack of 'christian' interest that I felt for the other three. I would have preferred them not to be there. I knew that Juliette couldn't be a lesbian, she was too stunning. I think I hoped she wasn't because then we could be friends. In any case, she was completely out of my league and half my age. I was no longer interested in dating men but the idea of openly dating a woman still terrified me. For thirty-odd years, I had believed that loving a woman was dangerous for the soul and would jeopardise my being accepted into normal society. That was not going to change overnight. I was still the most homophobic lesbian I knew.

We ambled out of the Universal Studios entrance. In keeping with the Chanel jacket, the diamond bracelet, and Versace handbag, Juliette got into a fat black Chevrolet with dark tinted windows. I hoped that she saw the roof descending on my convertible mustang, revealing my wrap-around shades and blond hair. I pulled out into the traffic faster than usual so that she could see me drive back past her. I looked straight ahead. I hoped that she would see my complete indifference, cultivated over years of disguising my attraction to women. At the Smoke House, I found out that Juliette was, in fact, a personal assistant, taking eight weeks off from floating around the world on her billionaire boss's ocean-going yacht.

"How's he managing without you?" I asked.

"Not great but this was the deal when I agreed to work for him, my life mostly isn't my own." Her phone interrupted us, "Hey Raffy…sure yes…!" She was coquettish and energised, "Tomorrow? No, I'll make my own way. Bye…! Yeah, see you then!" She hung up and winked at me, "That was Rafaello."

"Clearly," I laughed.

"He's Italian, and incredibly handsome."

"Great! We all need a handsome Italian."

I had the old familiar feeling. Here we go! Now I have to feign interest in her boyfriend.

"I've gone a bit crazy since I've been here," she continued, "being cooped up on the boat." The phone went again. "See what I mean?" She looked at the screen and sighed, "This one's rich, but not so handsome." She launched into the next conversation, "Hi Rob, how you doing? Lovely to hear from you!" she was looking at me with raised eyebrows. "Sure I enjoyed it too. Yes, tonight could work. Okay, call me when you get to my place!"

Later? It was already ten o'clock. I was completely exhausted from standing around for hours in a dress and high heels.

"Okay," she continued, "Pick me up in an hour, I need to get changed."

Get changed?! What life was she living? More to the point, what life was I living? Where had I been? Twenty-one years as a high school teacher had kept me shut in most nights, marking and preparing lessons.

She put the phone away again. I commiserated, "I feel for you. It must be terrible!" She laughed at my sarcasm and lowered her voice, "I'm juggling them all, it's actually becoming a nightmare. Maybe you could come along sometime!"

I clearly did the right thing to leave teaching! This was so much more exciting! I had once prayed for a more interesting life. My prayer had been answered, Juliette seemed keen to include me. "How about coming out with me, maybe Friday? I'm going out with Philippe. He's a producer, he's done big films and he hasn't hit on me yet—he might be fine with me bringing you. What do you think?"

"Sure, sounds fun." I was all in. She asked for my number. *Audrey Hepburn* just asked me for my number!

# CHAPTER TWENTY-SEVEN

That week, we continued to seek each other out and smoke on the roof (I didn't inhale). The lesbian martial arts acting teacher would whistle through her teeth as she passed me in the corridor, conveying her respect as well as a look of *you know you're playing with fire, don't you?* Fire was clearly what I wanted to play with.

I was relying on the fact that Juliette was straight but I was doing my high school behaviour of befriending the beautiful straight girl and suffering in silence. The upside to the suffering was the fact that everything about Juliette was glamorous and oh so Hollywood.

Friday couldn't come soon enough. She picked me up. She looked amazing. We went out to a restaurant way out in the valley. On arrival, the car was taken by the valet (I was still adjusting to paying someone to put the car where I could have put it myself.) We were led through a canopy of purple bougainvillea hanging over old wooden beams illuminated by uplighters. To reach our table we had to walk around a floodlit swimming pool. Heads turned and there were lingering looks on Juliette. People were doing the LA thing of trying to work out if she was a celebrity. For the uninitiated, a celebrity sighting instantly elevated one's status. We slid along opposite benches to face each other and took the menus handed to us by our waiter, a dark-eyed Adonis.

"Ladies, my name is Carlos, I'll be taking care of you tonight so please let me know if there is anything I can do for you. Philippe wants you to know that he is on his way and to just go ahead and order whatever you want."

I was thrilled at this news—that Philippe would be late and that I could order whatever I wanted! Philippe sounded like a big shot!

This all seemed very normal to Juliette. Without opening the menu she asked the waiter,

"Do you have rock oysters?" Rock oysters? Were there different kinds of oysters? I had tried oysters once as a child, whilst on holiday with my parents at Fisherman's Wharf in San Francisco. They were slimy and pointless and I had gagged following the instruction to swallow them whole.

Carlos responded, "We don't have rock oysters. However today we did get in some delicious West Coast Oysters and they come with Meyer lemon, borage, and caviar. I don't think you will be disappointed." West Coast of where I wondered, and what was a Meyer lemon and what was borage?! Sooo out of my depth!

"You okay with oysters Fiona?"

"Yes, how lovely!"

To the waiter she said, "We'll start with a dozen, thank you."

The oysters arrived and they were surprisingly delicious, not at all slimy as I remembered them and Audrey Hepburn chewed hers so I followed suit. So far so good. To follow, I chose the lamb, I hoped it was lamb chops but it turned out to be slices.

Philippe didn't arrive until the main course was well underway. He was tall, energetic and French, and very apologetic. He reminded me of a slimmed-down Gérard Depardieu.

"Hey girls! 'ow are you? Great to meet you Fiona, come 'ere Juliette, embrasse-moi!" He leaned over the bench and put his arms around her, "You're gorgeous you know that?! Isn't she gorgeous, Fiona? So what are we drinking? Want another one? Who's driving? We can always get you a cab and collect ze car tomorrow? How was acting class? Can't wait to get Mademoiselle Juliette onto ze big screen. She eez so beautiful? When will you be ready? We 'ave casting for a nice low-budget romcom starting in a month. Probably shoot out of Toronto. You think you will 'ave ze hang of the acting thing by then chérie? Not that it really matters, with a face like yours we can do anything with you. You should 'ave seen her on ze TV in France, Fiona. She was sensationelle!"

He barely stopped to take a breath. Juliette leapt in laughing, "You exaggerate, sérieusement!"

"Not really," he retorted, "remember when we were in St Tropez just after ze show ended, you and I could 'ardly get down ze street with all ze people stopping us and wanting your autograph!"

"It was a stupid TV show," she blurted, "no one here knows anything about it."

Philippe's blackberry vibrated, stopping his flow and he glanced down at it, "Merde! Forgive me girls I 'ave to take zees! Back in a sec!" Distracted, he walked off up the path, the blackberry pressed to his ear. When he returned, his voice sounded tight, "Girls, I 'ave a fifty million deal going south and I'm going to be fighting fires all night, so sorry, I 'ave to leave you, stay as long as you like. I'll settle up with Carlos later. Enjoy your night." He warmly took my face in his hands, kissed me on both cheeks, "Great to meet you, Lady Fiona! Juliette, I'll give you a bell and make zees up to you."

She stood up and he slipped his arm around her waist pulling her towards him and she put both arms around his neck, then ruffled his hair comfortingly as if he were ten and not forty-five. She pecked him on the lips then wiped off the lipstick with her thumb.

"Does he have a girlfriend?" I asked when he had gone.

"He does but it's a bit on and off, more off at the moment. We've known each other forever from Paris. He's just a friend."

Just a friend I thought, hmm, a really *friendly* friend.

"Anyway," she said, "have you got a boyfriend?"

Oh God, I was dreading this moment. I hated the way I usually fudged the answer. This time I wanted to do it differently. No more lying.

"Well," I spoke slowly, "I have had boyfriends," (I always said that because it was true but mostly because being bisexual sounded so much better than simply being gay.)

The wine arrived; Carlos showed the bottle to Juliette and then uncorked it and poured some into a glass for her to sample. She swilled and sniffed it then took a sip, "Hmm that's great, thanks." Carlos poured both glasses and we toasted and clinked them together.

"Eyes," she said, "you have to look at me when you do that."

So we clinked again and this time our eyes met, and she smiled that big perfect smile, "You were saying?"

I took a deep breath and blurted out, "Well, I just broke up with a woman." It was like jumping off a cliff.

Completely unfazed, she said, "I thought so. I knew it."

"What do you mean?"

She smiled, "I mean I knew you played both sides."

"Really? Damn! That obvious?" I was worried, I prided myself on being able to stay under the radar and it terrified

148          *Fiona Goodwin*

me to look obviously gay. It terrified me more to be outed. But Juliette didn't seem weirded out. "What's wrong with that anyway?" she asked. She wasn't bothered in the least.

"Well I'm not that comfortable about it and my last relationship was kept a secret for eleven years. I'm English." What kind of a pathetic excuse was that!

She followed that up with, "Well I've had my share of girls. My longest relationships have been with girls."

I reached for my wine and held the glass steadily as I slowly shook my head, "Now *that* I never would have guessed!"

There was silence, she was grinning. "I do have a tattoo!'

She was laughing at me, enjoying watching my reaction. I had no idea what was going on. I tried to play it cool, "Well, what an interesting night…"

The half-eaten lamb on my plate was looking less appetizing. I noticed how white the tablecloths were. I loved eating at a table with a starched, white tablecloth.

Juliette was enjoying my discomfort and we both sat back in our chairs to review our disclosures. I was curious, "But you have a *lot* of boyfriends now though?"

"Yeah, my boss introduced me to some producers and they introduced me to some casting agents. I'm just trying to get my career off the ground but mostly, I'm letting my hair down."

Again, I was curious, "You knew and you never said anything."

"Not my business to out you," she replied.

"Hmm. Good answer." I smiled, "shall we have some dessert?" I desperately wanted to muster some sense of control. Initiating dessert might do that. I chose an *ile flottante* and Juliette had a lemon tart.

I was beginning to breathe again and regain my composure. In fact, this was great, I was out, and Juliette was not only unconcerned but she seemed to be very comfortable being open about herself. I had never met a girl who had relationships with girls and who looked like a girl. In fact, I had never allowed myself to be friends with someone I thought might be gay.

On the contrary, Juliette seemed delighted, "Let's have a liqueur." This sounded celebratory. I had no clue what to have, hoping Juliette would come up with something, she did, "How about port and stilton?"

"Lovely!" I would have agreed to anything at this point.

From this moment, something changed between us, there was a complicity. I felt seen. Her lack of inhibition and acceptance of herself made me feel that I was breathing my own air, no longer skulking in the shadows. She shared her latest heartbreaks, I told her about Alexandra. She told me about the breakup with her girlfriend. I was fascinated by how she was dating all these different men. She said that she had not closed the door on men. More importantly, she wanted to act and she said that being with a lesbian was not the best recipe for a successful career in Hollywood. When she was acting in France, it wasn't a concern but here in Hollywood, it was a different story.

I confessed that I wished and had always wondered if I could be truly happy with a man. We talked about sex. For some unknown reason, I told her that I had never had a one-night stand. I had only been intimate with men or women whom I loved. I couldn't imagine giving my body over to someone who didn't really know or care about me.

She told me, "Well, sex can just be sex you know, and it's good to keep your hand in as it were!' she laughed.

I thought that having a one-night stand could be a way for me to shed some of my inhibition; maybe I could try separating sex from intimacy. We chatted on till there was no one left in the restaurant and Carlos asked us if he could close up the bill.

We drove home in a haze and when she dropped me off at my house I was floating and not even trying to fight off the ridiculousness of my infatuation. Waves of amazement and happiness washed over me. I realized I felt so much less alone. She seemed glad to find a kindred spirit and was slightly amused by my homophobia. I lay on my mattress on the floor and rehashed every word of our conversation, how she had come out at such a young age, and seemed not to carry any shame.

"It helped that I came out on national television," she had said, "they told me in the selection that the media would find out everything about me, especially the fact that I was living with my girlfriend, so I just took the plunge. There was no point lying and people were fine about it. My family already knew and they came on the show and said how proud they were of me and how much they liked my girlfriend. Even my grandmother came on. My family is just really broadminded."

I wondered what that must be like; having parents who accepted you instead of calling it "perversion" or my mother's favourite word, "unnatural." I recounted my experience of being exorcised at church; she thought it was hysterically funny, "Why the hell would you let them do that to you? I would have told them where to go!" I shrugged my shoulders. Wondering myself, "I honestly don't know. They were nice to me? They said they could cure me?" It took ages to get to sleep, my mind was racing.

I had to get up and make a cup of tea and put the TV on to wear myself out.

Jealousy met me head-on the next day at film school. She was joking and chatting during the break with a charming Norwegian student, Bjarne. So, I went off with some other students and reminded myself how insane I was, how I had no justification for these feelings, how this is how things always ended up, and I should get a grip and forget about her. Forget about her, like that was ever going to happen. Every time I caught a glimpse of her, my heart stopped. This was going to make the rest of my time at the school utterly miserable. I felt jilted and heartbroken after a few oysters and a piece of lamb! What a sick puppy I was! Moments like these, I thought, made me think that the Christians were right. I had a demon. I will never be normal, I will be forever tortured and why didn't I just get on that train and go back to the convent? What kind of life was this? Eternally damned to fall in love with girls and eternally damned to be unattracted to men. I practically threw myself out of the classroom door as soon as our scenes were done.

# CHAPTER TWENTY-EIGHT

Juliette's voice stopped me in my tracks as I swung the door wide onto the scorching hot street. "Hey Fi! Where are you going?"

"Oh hi," I said lamely.

"Where have you been all day? I saw you go for coffee then I couldn't find you." She sounded genuinely disappointed.

"Oh I went out," I said, "I had to make some calls." (Like I had calls to make!)

"Ok well just wanted to find out what you're doing Thursday night? Giancarlo is taking me out. Do you want to come? I asked him if I could bring a friend." Seeing my struggle to engage, she kept going, "I could really use a friend to go with me. It will be more fun if you're there. It makes me nervous going on my own, and he's Mafia and he's really into me.

Mafia?! That did it. She needed my protection. That's all it took to get me back in the game. "Sure, I'm free Thursday." I was changing my tune, warming up.

"Great, thanks!" And as she turned the other way down the street she added, "Oh and he has a French friend he wants you to meet, Antoine. Some guy who has brought his racehorses from France."

A Frenchman?! Races horses?! I wasn't at all sure how comfortable I was with this. In fact, I was totally uncomfortable with this. I had dated a physical education teacher and a telephone salesman—I had never met a man who raced horses, "Will he bring the horses?" I shouted back, an attempt at humour.

"No, but he might be good in the saddle!" She winked and laughed at my wide-eyed terror, "Maybe a good moment to get over that *one-night stand* thing!"

"Oh yes," I replied, fighting the desire to choke, "There's an idea!"

I should be grateful! I had read that the man who wrote *Men are from Mars and Women are from Venus*, had been a monk and when he left the priesthood, he had asked women if they would "teach" him—that's the sporting attitude! I must be more adventurous and experimental. My self-coaching was a little halfhearted but all I knew was that I would be spending the evening with Juliette and that she was good for me. I was uptight about sex and needed to let my hair down and not make such a big deal about it. Juliette was going to be a great help clearly but then again, what was I doing being with a man? Maybe if I met the right one? I did like horses. I was still on the fence apparently and willing to do literally anything to be near this gorgeous woman.

Thursday night came around quickly. Juliette picked me up, she looked even more like a movie star, "We are going to the Mondrian on Sunset" That meant nothing to me, it sounded like a bank. She noticed my blank face, "You'll love it! It's a club. We're meeting them there."

Meeting *them* there? This was a double date! A first. If only I had done less Bible study in my teens and twenties, and thirties, I would feel less terrified.

On arrival, a handsome young Latino guy in black

chinos and white polo shirt took the car and drove it down to the underground garage. I wasn't worried about the cost of the evening, when I was with Juliette, I never had to pay for anything—men were always fighting over the bill. The Mondrian was buzzing with hipness and cool beautiful people all looking around at the other cool beautiful people. There was a lot of glass and white sofas and then after some texting, Juliette led us outside to the blue floodlit pool, "He's taken a cabana," she beamed, "the fifth one along, "you have to spend at least six hundred dollars to have a cabana."

Hmm, a cabana, I looked over and thought they must be the white tents by the pool. What was in the cabana that made it cost six hundred dollars? They must be amazing! This was exhilarating. I was living the high life! I felt proud. People were looking at Juliette, she was turning heads. I threw my head back and laughed loudly when she pointed to Giancarlo. He was waving and smiling at us, a dark-haired Italian, about thirty years old. There was no need to laugh—I just wanted people to know I belonged, that I was having fun. On some level, I knew that these were astonishingly superficial thoughts. No one knew that I had been a trainee nun or that I had taught in inner-city high schools for twenty-one years. I had resigned from saving the world now; I was in Hollywood embracing the glamour and my own superficiality.

In the cabanas, I could see that it was going to be difficult to sit. There were two cream, deep-cushioned couches. Reclining seemed to be the thing to do. Giancarlo gazed into Juliette's eyes for way too long, holding her at the waist, "Amore, buona sera, sai che sei la piu bella donna nel mondo!" He was clearly besotted. Juliette looked deep into his eyes and I worried about the lipstick on his face as she planted a kiss on his lips but she wiped it off just as she had done with Philippe.

"Fiona speaks Italian," she said," I detected some pride, "oh and French. Talk to him in Italian, Fiona!'

I decided I should copy Juliette's approach and took his hands and quite uncharacteristically kissed this stranger on both cheeks, after all, if he was Mafia, I wanted him to like me. Under my breath, I translated, "He said you're the most beautiful woman in the world. I think he might like you!" Then I turned to Giancarlo, "Tante grazie Giancarlo per aver invitarmi stassera."

"Piacere" he replied, "and you too are beautiful, your Italian is perfect and we should really continue in Italian but then maybe Juliette will start to get jealous?"

We all laughed at the unlikelihood of that ever happening.

Juliette glowed with pride at my linguistic ability. Giancarlo lay down, propped up with cushions, and she lay beside him with her head against his chest. It looked terribly awkward to me and my own awkwardness at having no one to lean against was soon alleviated by the arrival of Antoine.

Antoine was not tall but had long flowing brown hair and piercingly dark eyes, he looked Middle Eastern. He was in his late thirties. Mimicking Juliette, I leaned against him on the couch. I could feel the muscles in his chest and arms.

"Fiona, speak to him in French!" Juliette suggested.

I obliged and after a few vodkas from what I learned was the six hundred dollar bottle, he eyed my cleavage and in heavily accented English said, "You are not plastique huh? You are naturelle, I cannot stand ze LA girls, zay are all plastique!" He seemed quite aggressively upset with LA girls, "Err, I always like ze European girls."

I was flattered.

A vodka later, he asked 'What are you doing after zees?'

What am I doing? It was late. I didn't know what the right answer was, "Well I will probably go home and have a hot chocolate and go to bed."

He smiled, "Well, we can go together back to my 'otel. I am free tomorrow. Zee 'orses need some time to settle in and get over ze jetlag."

Oh God, go back to his hotel?! Together? Horses with jetlag? Poor things, stuck in a plane for ten hours…

"Sounds great," I forced it out and comforted myself with his appreciation of my breasts. I looked for help from Juliette but she had now assumed maximum reclining position with Giancarlo. I was frightened but pleased with myself. Juliette might be impressed—she might like me more. I let a few minutes go by and my sipping of vodka had turned to swigging large gulps, this was inspired by the advice a few years back from the Jungian analyst who had recommended a large quantity of alcohol to loosen me up to be able to have sex with my Christian boyfriend for the first time. The strategy had been only partially successful but I didn't think I could get away with *partial success* with Antoine! My therapist had said that at thirty-five maybe I should throw anything and everything at helping me to lose my virginity. His advice was coming in handy now. I disentangled myself from Antoine and whispered in his ear in my sexiest voice, "Je m'excuse, je dois faire pipi." I had to go to the bathroom. I went over to Juliette who had come up for air, "Team talk, please! I need to talk to you NOW!"

"Sure. See you in a minute GC," and she slowly kissed her index finger and then ran it down his nose and over his lips and with all the coquettishness of a sixteenth-century courtesan, "Don't go away!" He made a sad face and she made a sad face back.

She got up and we made our way to the completely mirrored bathroom. Juliette gazed in the mirror and reapplied her lipstick, "What's up? Are you having fun? It's going well right?" She seemed delighted for me.

"He wants me to go home with him," I was boasting, "I have to be fifteen years older than him!" I said that for emphasis.

She stopped looking in the mirror and seemed excited for me, "That's great!" she said, "but why don't you come back to mine? Just in case? You'll feel safer, I don't like the idea of you being on your own with him. We don't even know who he is!"

Good point, I thought. That hadn't crossed my mind. My anxiety was mostly to do with not knowing what I was doing. I didn't want to look stupid, and I didn't want my inexperience to reflect badly on Juliette.

She explained what should happen, "Giancarlo and I will be in my bed, and you and 'ze 'orseman can 'ave ze couch!'" She laughed. It was so matter of fact, this was going to be easy! Juliette would be in the other room "just in case." Just in case of what? I thought. Well, never mind that. I was so grateful to Juliette for taking care of me. We would be together, sort of. We laughed raucously as we walked out of the bathroom, and people looked at us.

As we threaded our way back through the deafening thud thud of the music and the dark shadows of the gyrating bodies on the dance floor, Juliette stopped in her tracks. She swung around to face me and held me by the shoulders. She yelled in my ear, "It's so 'ot…" I couldn't hear the end of the sentence,

"Yes, it's incredibly hot!" I yelled back.

"No," she shouted, "it's so 'ot when you talk French!" She smiled and stared right into my eyes.

I was embarrassed, "Thanks!" I shouted back, "In England, we get taught…" I was about to launch into a treatise on the merits of the British education system but my words were cut off as she took my face in both her hands and moved towards me. I felt the warmth of her lips, I wondered about the lipstick, she kissed me full on the mouth, I realized I didn't care about the lipstick. And I didn't care that these were the same lips that had been kissing Giancarlo from the Mafia, a few minutes earlier. This wasn't a kiss of convenience, the kiss lingered. I was almost too shocked to respond, it happened so quickly. Everyone would be watching us (I hoped.) Good Lord! What was happening? She pulled back and laughed at my bewildered face, she wiped the lipstick away with her finger, and then with the emphasis on *really* she shouted, "Reeelly 'ot!"

I was almost too happy to speak, and a little shy. I thought, "This is Hollywood. I'm in a movie. The most beautiful girl in the world just kissed me in a chic nightclub on Sunset Boulevard in front of hundreds of complete strangers. She is kissing me, the nun, the schoolteacher with bad teeth. I could hear angels and the Metro Goldwyn lion roar. Nothing else mattered anymore, this was what I had been waiting for. Tonight, this year, forever…

I smiled a little sheepishly, "At this moment in time, that's quite confusing!" She laughed, "It is, isn't it! Come on! Let's go back to the men!" I followed and wanted to glance to see if anyone was watching or applauding even, but I just kept my gaze on the flowing dark hair bobbing its way to the edge of the dance floor.

We were both flushed with excitement on arrival and I was looking forward now to going back to her flat. It was as if we were going to go back there to be together, so strange.

"Let's go," she said to Giancarlo.

"Sure." he smiled. She turned to Antoine, "Why don't you and Fi come back to my place? Save you getting a cab, and there's a couch…"

"Pas de problème!" He was happy.

I don't remember much about the ride home. I do remember as I went through Juliette's front door, she handed me a small packet, "You might need this."

Oh God! I had never been in charge of a condom before. I thought it was the man's job to provide the equipment. Then I remembered, when I was teaching, I had occasionally taught sex ed. Using a Jaguar gear stick (which is modeled on a penis apparently) I taught teenage girls and boys how to put on a condom. So it wasn't exactly the first time I had been in charge of one.

"Thanks," I grinned ruefully. She was thoughtful as well as beautiful and here I was about to spend the night with someone from the Mafia, I had a condom in my hand, and I couldn't wait for breakfast!

Thankfully, it was already 3 a.m. by the time we arrived at her apartment right by the film school. Juliette laid a sheet and blanket on the narrow sofa and I felt scared and sad as she turned to go. I kept up a brave front. She looked so pleased for me. Antoine took all his clothes off but I crawled under the blanket, provided by Juliette, in my bra and pants. Once he joined me, they were swiftly and efficiently removed. He had done this before, clearly. There was no conversation, no tender words. This was a one-night stand, I reminded myself. I'm a grown woman now and this is what grown women do.

I hadn't stayed in the convent; I had opted for the real world. If I wanted to play with the big girls, I needed to get with the programme. I had never played with the girls anyway. What made me think I could ever be one of them? There was very little foreplay before he lay on top of me and I wondered when would be the right time to hand him the small packet that I had secreted under the brown velvet cushion that my head lay on? For safety I decided to give it to him immediately, I reached under the pillow and showed it to him,

"That's there if you need it?" *If* you need it? Shouldn't I have said *when* you need it? *If* implied that it was optional. It wasn't optional but I was secretly hoping that he wouldn't need it.

"Merci." He grabbed it and ripped the packet open with his teeth. I closed my eyes as he fumbled with it and then almost immediately he seemed to turn into a grunting pneumatic drill pushing his erection into me. That was good I thought, he was hard which I hoped was because he was attracted to me. I didn't let him in, couldn't let him in, I felt aroused but there was no way that I was going to let him inside me and not just because of the size of him. He was athletic and kept trying. I had to give him full marks for effort and to be fair, I was slightly aroused but mentally and emotionally, I was completely detached. I was wondering what Juliette was doing, feeling sad that I was there with the unknown French horse racer and she was next door with the handsome Italian gangster. I felt guilty for not knowing how to participate. He was making all this effort and I was just lying there like a corpse. I really didn't know what to do and let's face it, my heart wasn't in it. I had no desire to join in and as he pushed down on me ever more forcibly, I wondered if this was how it felt to be assaulted. I couldn't wait for it to be over. It was starting to hurt. To my amazement, the friction of him rubbing against me made me come, and confusingly that's when I heard the bedstead from Juliette's bedroom start to rhythmically bang on the wall behind my head. It gained momentum. It was distracting and intimidating. A crescendo was reached and there were groans and moans, and then silence. Antoine gave up the gymnastics and rested his head on my bare, but *real* breasts, and I felt extraordinarily relieved and inadequate. If I were a proper woman I would ask him what he wanted but there was no way I was going to do that. I wouldn't know what to do and I was exhausted. Apart from anything, what was I doing having sex with him in the first place? Unbelievably I must still be harbouring hopes of being straight? I feigned sleepiness and he seemed comfortable and quiet, resting his head on my chest like an exhausted puppy.

Waking the next morning, I was glad to have ticked off the *one night stand*. I didn't need to do that again, especially when the person I wanted to be with was in the adjoining room making the earth move with someone else. Oh dear, what a familiar scenario this was, hearing someone I loved, make love to someone else. I wasn't the chosen one. I was the bystander, the spectator, the outsider. I didn't ever want to stop feeling or to die feeling nothing, and I wasn't sure if my heart could withstand unendingly being discounted. The sideline was not a neutral place to be, it was jammed with rage and envy and utterly excruciating isolation. I wondered if I would die prematurely just by dint of the number of times my heart had been broken simply by being overlooked. People die of broken hearts. Is there a moment when it reaches critical mass and it just says "enough?" because the ventricles are too worn out from trauma?

The next morning, we didn't speak as we folded the blanket and sheet. He wandered off to the bathroom. Poor man, I didn't want him to feel he hadn't done a good job. I wondered what he would say to Giancarlo, "What a useless lump of meat you found me!?" And then I wondered if he had been told in advance that he was fulfilling a lifelong ambition of mine to have a one-night stand.

Juliette appeared tousled and relaxed, "How was it?"

I had no idea what to say or worse, who I was saying it for, "It was a one-night stand I guess," I smiled wanly, "It was fine," I continued, sounding chirpy, a lot like my mother, "What an athlete! Amazing physique! Quite a night!" I quickly turned the subject to her, "and great to have a grandstand seat for your night with Giancarlo!"

"Yes the walls are really thin," she was unabashed "and you were doing a fair amount of panting yourself!"

"Was I?" I didn't remember much, "I was probably trying to draw breath with the weight of the Frenchman on top of me."

"So not great then?" She queried. I wanted to say, "Well I was in the wrong room so it was never going to be great!" I didn't say that of course. I didn't want to appear ungrateful so I cheerily said, "No, it was great. I would have liked to have been a little more warmed up I think."

"Ah," she understood that, "he was a bit too quick off the mark then? You should have said something."

"Said something? What was I going to say? The man races horses!"

"Whoah Neddy?!" she bantered back, breaking into laughter.

"You're probably right, I'll bear that in mind for next time." I smiled. On the way to breakfast, Antoine and I chatted idly, as if he hadn't just failed to penetrate me.

That Thursday night, a miracle occurred. I actually forgot Juliette for three whole hours. I was downtown at the Ahmanson Theater watching Lynn Redgrave (Vanessa Redgrave's sister) performing her one-woman show. I was able to go backstage to meet Ms. Redgrave and Miriam Margolyes at the Stage Door. I felt a longing, a ferocious longing to be the one on stage, bearing my soul and cracking them up with one-liners, but my thoughts turned to Juliette as soon as I was in the car driving home. The phone went. It was her, "How do you fancy a coffee?"

"What, now?" I asked, "it's eleven o'clock!"

"I know," she laughed, "I'm staying in tonight! Having the night off!"

She calls eleven o'clock a "night off?!" The steering wheel turned all by itself, off the 101 freeway and back towards her apartment, "Sure, I'll see you in a few."

Coffee late at night seemed a really bad idea but I soon got my head around the thought of a nice hot drink.

This was my first time back to the apartment since my night of "passion" with Antoine, Giancarlo, and Juliette. This time we would be alone. I was overjoyed. On my arrival, she phoned down to the gate and the attendant waved me in. I noticed the luxuriousness of her suite—shiny granite countertops and under-floor lighting, glaring sophistication.

"We may as well have a proper drink." She winked at me as she opened the mahogany drinks cabinet. With eyebrows raised, I nodded, and sarcastically said, "Absolutely, we may as well." What happened to the coffee I thought? And what about driving? But I knew one small drink wouldn't hurt.

She smiled and presented me with a chunky glass of vodka, clinking with ice and lemon.

"Cheers," I sipped and nearly choked. "This is strong!"

She laughed, "It will do you good!"

It will, I thought. She was right. This is good for me. I was finally letting my hair down. I didn't have the nerve to perform on stage but at least I could knock back a vodka at 11 p.m. on a Thursday night. This was unheard of in my teaching days. Getting to bed early was the only way to survive the daily grind.

Juliette sat down next to me, close. The television was on some random crime detection programme, the story of a serial killer being tracked down.

"We don't have to watch this," she had noticed my eyes widening at the reenactment of the discovery of body parts in a deep freezer. I was nervous, "No it's fine." I remained fixed on the screen. "Yes this show is awful, and this vodka is going straight to my head… and you are sitting *reeeeeelly* close!"

Laughing she replied, "Sorry is that's bothering you?" She moved a little closer.

"No… no….not really." My voice tapered off. I sounded pathetic. I wondered if I should tell her about the play and meeting Ms. Redgrave and Miriam Margolyes but Juliette's proximity and the rising body count on the television were distracting.

"I'll switch it off," she said. She moved towards the television and I noticed the skinny blue jeans and the see-through chiffon peach blouse. Some kind of incense was burning. She put on some music that I didn't recognize, a slow sultry beat. When she sat back down, our thighs were touching. I was grateful for the vodka that was softening the edges of my anxiety and absolving me from any crime that I might commit.

"Drink up!" She encouraged me as I played with my glass and only occasionally took small sips. Years of abstinence whilst following Jesus meant I was no match for the large tumbler. I did as I was told and drank it back. I didn't know any more if I was taking the *medicine* out of compliance or collusion but I was very grateful when after not much conversation she said, "I think we would be more comfortable in the bedroom, don't you? In fact, you should probably stay the night—I don't think driving would be a good idea now?"

How practical. It made sense. I was a happy lamb, being led willingly to slaughter. I didn't care less if I got chopped up and put in a freezer. She took my hand and led me to the bedroom. The lighting was low, thank God—I didn't want her to see my body.

"Here, I have a t-shirt Giancarlo left behind the other night." She held out the man's shirt.

"Oh, great thanks." This shirt had good karma.

She went into the bathroom and closed the door. I hastily threw off my clothes, put on the large white Nike t-shirt, and jumped into bed. I felt the luxuriousness of the Egyptian cotton as my head sank into the fluffy pillow. I lay staring at the ceiling, She reemerged wearing frilly baby pink shorts and a smock loosely laced at the front. She climbed into bed and lent on her left elbow with her head on her hand, always smiling, "Wow you really are a lightweight, aren't you Fifi."

"Yep." I pursed my lips. *Fifi* sounded so hot, no one called me Fifi.

"One vodka," I continued, "and I'm…"

"Anybody's?!" She laughed and slid her hand across my

stomach around my waist. "I'm not anybody," she warmly reproached me.

"No, I'm kinda getting that…"

She moved towards me and very tenderly put her lips on mine. Her long curls fell across my forehead. She was so gentle, so stunningly beautiful. When she pulled back, I was smiling, "I'm not feeling so sleepy now."

"Nor me," she reached to the bottom of my t-shirt, "You're not going to need this after all." And pulled it up over my head.

I surrendered, then tried to gather my thoughts, "You should probably take off your pyjamas then?" I sounded awkward, like a nurse about to conduct a medical examination.

"No, I like the feel of them on me."

"Oh ok." Out of my depth again, so out of my depth!

"Fifi, you should probably stop talking now…"

I nodded, pressed my lips together to signal obedience, and then reached up and kissed her on the cheek and felt the cotton of her pyjamas against my naked skin and thought how good cotton felt and how good she felt.

"I might not be very good at this," I blurted out, "It's been a while and I've never been with a French teenager…" I was trying to joke away my nerves.

"Fifi you agreed to shut up…"

"Did I?"

She stopped me with her lips and leaned over me, pinning my wrists to the bed. She lifted herself up to study my eyes. "Your eyes are the first thing I noticed about you. So blue, you must have been told that a lot."

"Not really…" I felt awkward not knowing how to respond.

Juliette looked shocked, "Wow, they are amazing," and she came closer and whispered in my ear, "And I DIDN'T say you could talk…"

I didn't talk again, not till the following morning, and even when I came to with the smell of freshly ground coffee wafting in the air. I was silent, wondering if it had all been a dream.

"Hey you, Englishwoman." She was standing by the bed in a full-length red silk kimono. A tray of croissants and a cafetière of coffee were carefully lowered onto the bed-side table next to me. There was a posy of blue and yellow flowers in a small vase. She sat on the edge of the bed and took a blue flower out of the vase and touched it to my lips, "This is for you."

I pulled myself up and rubbed my eyes.

"Thank you, French girl." I took the flower and put it to up to my nose. "This is lovely, my colours," and glancing at the tray, "all of it."

"Move over," she said. I moved over and she removed her dressing gown and climbed into bed next to me. Self-conscious at my nakedness, I found Giancarlo's t-shirt and pulled it over my head.

"You didn't have to do that," she said.

"Oh yes I did, daylight requires it!"

She passed me a plate with a warm croissant and then poured coffee with fresh cream.

"This is the best birthday EVER!" I announced.

"It's your birthday?!" She reeled. "You never said!"

"I clearly didn't need to!"

"Wow, you kept that quiet! Birthdays are *so* important!"

"Not really. That's sweet of you, but not really."

She munched on her croissant, brow furrowed, and

then she lit up. "I know what…! We have a long lunch break today. I'm going to take you to Sushi Dan. Do you like sushi?"

"I don't know, I've never had it."

"Perfect!" She was delighted with her plan. "We better get moving. Class starts in an hour. Leave some room for lunch!"

The spare croissants were whisked away to the kitchen, "And leave your car here!" she shouted from the shower, "we'll take mine."

It was indeed the best birthday I had ever had, right up until the moment we were finishing the meal at Sushi Dan.

"I have to go to Milan tomorrow. Jean Luc, my boss, has meetings so I'm taking the day off school. I have to pack tonight…" she said the words slowly.

My heart sank. Milan, she's going away, she won't be at school. I tried to sound casual, "How long are you going for?"

"Just a long weekend, back Monday night. I don't really want to go but I can't get out of it."

"That's a shame…" I tried to sound sympathetic but felt desolate. The rug had been pulled and my stomach was on the floor. My perfect birthday had crashed. We returned to school slightly inebriated and back in the classroom, I forced a smile.

Class ended and she drove me back to get my car. I had to get my forlorn face away from her. I felt like a six-year-old. I faked a cheery, "Have a great time. See you when you get back," and gave her a sisterly hug on the pavement.

She looked askance, "You're not going to come up for a drink then?"

"No, thanks, you should get on with your packing."

"Ok", she hesitated, "well enjoy the rest of your day."

"Thanks! And thanks for an amazing lunch!"

"Sure", then quizzically, "you know this weekend is not what I most want to do right now?"

I leaned out of the car window, embarrassed by my desolation, "Thanks, that's good to hear."

She grabbed my arm and reached into the window and kissed me on the lips. "See you soon! Tuesday in class for God's sake!" She smiled the smile and my heart melted a little.

That weekend was torture. I went running every day alongside the waterless, concreted Los Angeles River. Its desolation perfectly mirrored my own. The sound of Sia in my headphones singing, "Breathe" offered little comfort.

Juliette came to find me at school on the following Tuesday and we went back to her apartment. She unbuttoned her jacket, "Look at this…" She showed me a diamond and emerald necklace.

"Oh my God, how many diamonds is that?!"

"Twenty-five thousand dollars-worth." She looked thrilled and sheepish.

"From your boss?!"

"Yes."

"Wow! I don't know any boss that gives that kind of gift."

Juliette's face crumpled, "I couldn't tell you before…"

"Couldn't tell me what?"

"You better sit down. I've been dreading telling you this. I haven't been completely truthful. When I was seventeen, I was travelling with my parents in Morocco. One morning, I left the hotel by myself and wandered through the bazaar. Out of nowhere, he appeared. He introduced himself, we made friends over a few days and he offered me all sorts of opportunities, promised to take care of me. From that moment on he has been in my life. I love him but not in a romantic way. I'm trying to leave so that I can stay in LA."

"In other words, you are a *kept woman?* I couldn't hide my hurt and disappointment.

"Yes, I'm taken care of," She burst into tears.

She left town with him half a dozen times over the next few months and phoned me, miserable, from penthouse suites all over the world. I was heartbroken, missing her terribly but she assured me that she was doing everything she could to get away. On top of my disappointment, I was also stressed, facing the challenge of making a living, alone in Los Angeles. My drive to do stand-up comedy and film acting were waning. The quandary of how to be with Juliette overtook my every waking hour. It was all I cared about. I had found the freedom to love a woman for the first time and I couldn't turn the clock back.

Juliette started including me in her glitzy lifestyle. I was flown to London, Paris, Japan, Rome. Each time, my luggage would be whisked away by a hotel valet and replaced by a glass of Veuve Cliquot. I had palatial hotel suites all of my own, mostly with Juliette and Jean Luc adjacent. At night-time, there would be a turndown service and a chocolate truffle placed on my pillow. I would eat it forlornly—a pathetic consolation prize. I knew there was something terribly wrong with this picture and I knew I had lost any connection to my ambition to perform. Now my ambition had shifted, I was on a mission. I was going to rescue this "maiden" if it was the last thing I did.

# CHAPTER TWENTY-NINE

The answer to the dilemma of how I was going to stay in Los Angeles and support myself came with a call from my friend Susan Dobson, wife of TV star Kevin Dobson who, for many years had played Bobby Crocker on Kojak. Susan and Kevin had kindly taken me in a year earlier when I contracted pneumonia living on the boat in the Marina. If I had asked the boat owner, I would have found out that there heating on the boat but being British I presumably felt it too rude to ask!

"Fiona, I know you are looking for an opportunity," she continued, "so why don't you come for drinks tonight?" There's an industry event at the House of Blues. It'll be fun and I'll introduce you to some people. It's black-tie by the way." Black tie? Fancy! Susan was always looking out for me.

We arrived around 9 p.m. and in heels and lipstick, we clambered up the wooden stairs to the VIP room at the top of the iconic building on Sunset Boulevard, sadly no longer there. The drinks were free and I had not eaten so the lychee martini knocked me for six. As Susan had some business to attend to, I wandered dangerously alone and tipsy amongst the spiffed-up Hollywood executives. I overheard a London twang from a silver-haired, distinguished David Putnam look-alike.

"Hello! I'm Fiona. I couldn't help hearing your lovely accent," I cheerily put my hand out, "you look really important! Who are you?"

He grinned and with perfect diction, uttered a decisive, "Fuck off," and walked away. His young colleague was left standing in front of me.

"Oops! Well, who was that!?" I was undeterred.

"No-one important," he replied, "just John Daly, the producer of a few Oscar-winning films such as Platoon and The Last Emperor." He was openly laughing at me.

"Oh shit!" I was mortified but the mojito had kicked in in a big way. I headed off again in search of my new friend John. I found him by the *hors d'oeuvres.*

"Mr. Daly, I just found out how important you are!" and quickly followed that up with, "Are you married?"

He looked slightly bemused but grinned, "No, no one will have me now."

"Ah," I replied, "well your luck has changed, because I'm here, and I need a green card. How about it?"

"Well, you really can fuck off now!" He smiled and off he went again with a plate of smoked salmon and a refill of sauvignon blanc.

Still, the mojito was doing its work. Armed with a plate of canapés I went in pursuit, "John, can I call you John? I apologise! I realise it's way too soon to talk about marriage, but I tell you what, if you give me a job, I promise I will never mention the M word ever again! You can't say fairer than that!' I smiled my best sexy mojito smile.

"Oh for fuck's sake! Tim?" we were now back with his young colleague. "She won't leave me alone. Have her come in to the office on Monday."

Susan found me at the end of the evening, "Did you

have fun?" My head was clearing by this time as I reran the conversation with her, "I think I might have just got the proverbial 'big break in Hollywood!'" She screamed with delight. "Oh my God Fiona! That's insane!"

And it was.

That Monday I showed up, now sober and terrified, at the plush offices of Film and Music Entertainment on Wilshire Boulevard. Security directed me to the silent elevator and emerging on the twenty-third floor there was a perfect view through the floor-to-ceiling glass, of the Hollywood sign. I was hired!

The first time I manned the reception, I was given a stern lecture by John, "Always check the security camera before you buzz anyone in. I've got some Russians after me and we really don't want them in here. They don't understand the business and they've got it into their heads that I owe them three million." Then he hesitated, "Having said that they'll have machine guns so those doors probably won't stand up to them." He wasn't joking.

May of the following year John sent me as part of the sales team to the Cannes Film Festival. I knew nothing about selling films.

"You speak French and Italian, you'll be fine," he reassured me, "It's no different from selling houses. Just don't make any decisions without Blayze's say-so. (Blayze was my stunning younger counterpart) "Oh and watch out for the Russians."

"The ones with the machine guns?" I was worried.

"No, different Russians. They will try to beat you down on price—it's because of the pirating, it's hard for Russian sales agents to recoup their money."

Landing at the airport in Nice, a black car was waiting

for us. I wondered if I was dreaming. How did I go from the convent to the jungle, to the inner city classroom, to becoming a Hollywood film sales executive?" It was my first big *acting* job! I bought Gucci sunglasses for the occasion. I had a business card that made people instantly want to be my *friend*. And Cannes was everything I imagined it to be. At night, there were mansions and palaces lined with flaming torches, awash with lobster and champagne and filet mignon. I smiled to myself thinking about the school teacher parties with plastic cups and economy bags of salt and vinegar crisps. I forgave myself for being so ridiculously dazzled by the sight of Brad and Angelina making their entrance on the red carpet in an explosion of flashing light bulbs.

And always in the back of my mind was Juliette. Thankfully she agreed to join me. It was hard to be fully present in anything without her being there.


Calamity struck however a few months after the Cannes Film Festival. I was in Paris, on a break from work, staying at the home of Jean Luc. Juliette and I had tickets to the Moulin Rouge. We had drinks after the show and whilst we were usually very careful out in public we were emboldened by the champagne and the flamboyance of the dancers so much so that in the back of the limo we kissed not noticing that the window to Victor, the chauffeur, was slightly open. The next morning we were out for breakfast and there was a message on Juliette's phone. She was ashen. "He knows something."

"How can he?" I replied reassuringly.

"Well, he must. He's furious! He says I have to go home immediately if I want somewhere to sleep tonight."

Juliette frantically called him and denied any wrongdoing. She told him that Victor had imagined it. Jean Luc was devastated and Juliette was white with fear. We abandoned our ritual of coffee and croissant and stood on the pavement to hail a taxi. I wanted to throw up in the gutter. She was at risk, she said. She might lose his support and any hope of her coming to LA would be dashed.

We didn't exchange a single word in the cab. She let me out close to the house, near Montmartre, "You can't come back here. Don't phone me. It's not safe. God knows what he would do to you."

I sat on the bench near the house where she left me for five long hours. I wanted to be there for her in case she was thrown out. It was starting to get dark and I was cold. My phone eventually rang. It was one of Juliette's American friends, she was a part of Jean Luc's entourage, "Hi Fiona, it's Jamie! Heard what happened. Sounds a bit shit. Juliette told me to come and find you. Some of us are having a drink. Write down this address, get a cab and come and meet us."

There were four exotic-looking women enjoying cocktails when I arrived at the bar. I was introduced. Two of them were Jean Luc's P.A.s. I got a cool reception.

"How is she?" was my first question.

"It's touch and go," was Jamie's response, "this is tough for her to explain. All your stuff, by the way, has gone in the dumpster. He's as mad as. You can't go anywhere near her or the house."

My visa and passport were in my suitcase! How was I going to get back to America?! If I didn't get back soon, I would lose my job. The other girls barely acknowledged me.

"You'll have to find somewhere to stay. Have a drink then I'll take you where you might get cheap accommodation."

I ordered a coffee and cradled it trying to get my hands warm. Conversation was stunted. When my coffee was finished, Jamie took me out to her car. As we drove she explained, "They all think that you deliberately let Victor see you guys kissing to get Juliette away from Jean Luc. Did you?"

"Not that I know of." That sounded lame. I had had all day to think about how this had happened.

"Maybe you did it unconsciously?" she asked.

"I don't think so—the last thing I wanted was to wreck her life and hurt Jean Luc."

She raised her eyebrows in disbelief, "I'll drop you here, it's not a great area but cheap. Don't stand around on the street. You'll get arrested."

I wandered towards Place Pigalle. I had so little money. She had dropped me off in the red light district. I had come a long way from the convent, that's for sure.

Fifteen euros a night got me a tiny garret, five floors up with a bathroom shared with six others. There was a security code to get into the hostel. C2XV1. I mustn't forget it. I sat bent over on the bottom bunk for ages clutching my knees, shell-shocked, wondering what was happening to Juliette, what would happen to me now that I had no way to get back to the US. I pictured my visa and passport in the dumpster in the discarded luggage. I heard nothing from anyone that night. I barely slept from the devastation and the constant noise of drunken girls shouting and staggering up and down the corridor.

The horror hit hard when I awoke. I heard from no one all day, and nothing all the next day. I didn't dare phone and in those days there was no such thing as texting. I was befriended by the working girls as each day, for ten days, I lined up at the phone box on the corner of the street, that's after one of them, Camille, offered me her services, "I do both, you know!"

Oh my God, it really was obvious! Being identified as gay was still so shaming, "Thank you I'm just waiting to use the telephone."

I could not make international calls on my mobile phone, and local calls were seventy cents a minute. Ten euro coins were rapidly swallowed up by calls to LA. Only my most broadminded friends were privy to the mess I was in. My acting teacher, Maria Gobetti, was horrified, "You should go to the American embassy."

"What can they do?" I protested, "I'm British, they'll send me back to the UK!"

"Well your visa and passport have been stolen, you should report Jean-Luc to the French police!"

"I can't. This is all my fault and it will get Juliette into trouble."

"Can you hear yourself, Fiona? She's got a roof over her head! You need to save yourself! You're stranded for God's sake!"

I was trying to focus on her words as I watched through the glass as Camille was led away by the French police. She was high. She shouted as she headed for the van, "A demain cherie, bonne chance avec le retour!" She was wishing me good luck with my return. I felt my eyes fill with tears from her kindness. Everything was topsy-turvy. It was dawning on me, albeit slowly, that I really was in trouble. I was running out of credit on my phone and running out of money. I managed on a baguette a day and a packet of mortadella. That was breakfast, lunch, and dinner. It was too expensive to buy coffees, so I bought a plastic bottle of water and kept filling it from the tap at the hostel. In any case, being confined to my bunk was comforting. Every day I wrote. My primitive, angst-filled garret was the perfect refuge for a searing inventory: how had my life come to this? C2XV1. I mustn't forget it. I mustn't forget any of this. Why was my journey characterized by tragic love affairs and hiding and an abdication of my own values and intentions? The cigarette smoke coming under my door felt like a necessary, additional punishment. Someone was smoking outside the room. Smoking was not allowed in the hostel. I wanted to report them. I wanted to say that it was because I didn't like the smell but that would have been a lie. I simply wanted to report someone, to have them punished and put into solitary confinement, just as I had been as a child, just as I was now. This was horribly familiar.

On the third day, Juliette finally phoned. She whispered, "I can't talk for long, he'll be back soon. Meet me in the park behind the Commissariat at two."

She arrived pale and gaunt. She seemed slightly out of it. Heavy doses of Xanax, she said. She whipped out a brown paper bag containing a small bottle of vodka. She offered me a swig. I took a sip to oblige.

"It's been days of listening to Jean Luc ranting and crying. I think he believes me now, that you are a crazy person, that you seduced me. His PA's are saying that this was your plan to get me away from him."

I was relieved for her that she had regained his trust and devastated that she had been turned against me. I had been cast as the villain. Now that I knew she would be safe, I had to get away but how could I without a passport and visa?

Over the next few days, she visited when she could. As her terror of eviction subsided, her trust and warmth returned. On day five she phoned me, "Get a taxi. Come to the back of the house at three. He should be out, but in case he isn't, when you get here, lie down on the backseat. If he sees you, he will kill you. I got your suitcase out of the dumpster. I'll throw it in the boot of the car!"

Phew! The relief! The "hit and run" was executed successfully. I had everything I needed to get home and I was finally able to catch a flight back to LA. It was strangely sad to leave my hideaway in Place Pigalle.

I returned to L.A. and immersed myself in just about every twelve-step programme that would have me—especially Co-dependent's Anonymous. I pined for Juliette and when I attempted to end our relationship in an email, she would not hear of it, "You can't break up with me in an email, not now that I am about to get away from here! You have to at least give us a chance. We've never had a chance at a normal life!"

She was right but my heart could no longer stand the uncertainty of this long distance relationship. "Well, you're not here and I have to get on with my life." That felt cold, but I was attempting to make my wellbeing a priority.

# CHAPTER THIRTY

onths later, my friend, Monica, called me. Her band was going to be playing in West Hollywood at a Gay Pride event. West Hollywood, I learned, was where all the *high-powered lesbians* lived. I had to move on and meet other women and this seemed like a good way to do it. Shoulder to shoulder in the crowd, I surveyed the scene. It was my first Pride Parade. I was moved to tears by the women openly holding each other's hands, openly expressing affection. If only I were brave enough to do that!

I scanned the crowd for the woman of my dreams. She was nowhere to be seen. I said to Monica's fifteen-year-old, "This isn't going to work! There's no one here for me." But, as my eyes surveyed the stage, I felt wistful, "I'd date any of the women in the band."

Monica's daughter clarified, "Well they're all married— to men. Except for the bongo player, she's got cats."

At the end of the gig, I was helping to load up the equipment when I found standing in front of me, the bongo player, "Hey! Fiona right? What are you doing tonight? Wanna come for dinner?"

There was something about her, she had incredibly muscular arms, from playing the bongos I expect. She was about my age, not an ounce of fat on her. Lovely white teeth and she looked funky in her black waistcoat, tight jeans, manicured nails.

"Lovely, thank you." I was grateful for the invite. I took Monica aside, "The bongo player with the lovely teeth has invited me to dinner!"

"Oh my God! Blair? You know she's gay, right?"

"She's gay?!"

"Yeah, kind of in the closet but she likes women."

I immediately wondered, was she the *one*? We drove up Laurel Canyon. I saw the spectacular view from her spectacular house. It must be her! I went to unload the bongos, but she was reluctant to let anyone touch them. I took charge. I was confident I knew how to handle Blair's bongos.

We were greeted at the door by her cats. They were designer rescue cats. It took a good twenty minutes to feed them because of the combination of wet food, dry food, two different flavour tins, all mixed with water to the correct consistency.

Then it was time to feed me. She whipped up some spinach and garlic and steak—no carbs obviously. She poured me a big glass of vodka. We ate and talked. She had a proper job, she was a TV executive—this was unusual in my circle of friends who were mostly semi-employed actors. I went home and the next day I phoned her to ask her out for coffee. My heart skipped a bit when I heard her voice, "I'm running out now, you'll have to call me when I have my calendar."

That threw me, "Well that's going to be difficult because I'm not going to know when you've got your calendar. How about you call me?

I got a text that night. "I don't drink coffee, and I don't text, would you like to come for dinner Saturday night?"

"Lovely," I wrote back. "Thank you. Anything I should bring?" She wrote, "Two pounds of freshly caught wild Atlantic salmon from Gelson's. You know the Gelson's on Franklin? If you go there and they don't have it, drive to the Whole Foods on Santa Monica and Fairfax, they should have it."

Not bad, I thought, for someone who didn't text. This woman knows exactly what she wants! I liked that. Besides, it was all very eye-opening for me. I'd never been into the world of expensive fish, or for that matter, expensive Hollywood lesbians. The fish cost forty-two dollars.

Date night arrived. I shaved my legs. My heart was pounding. I drove up the hill having secured the fish. I have to get better at this dating thing! Blair had left nothing to chance. We had dinner, there was music, low lighting, candles, I was thinking, "This is it. The house is sooo nice...!" But then my hopes fell as she pushed her plate away,

"I don't know what to do with you." I was baffled, "What do you mean you don't know what to do with me?" She barely made eye contact, "You're not really my type." That stung, but holding my own, I replied truthfully, "Well if it's any help, you're not really my type either." She was clearly taken aback, "Really?! Well what I mean to say is that you are not what I would usually go for, but when I think about holding you in my arms, I get wet."

'Get *wet*?!' I had never heard that expression before. Was she referring to her bottom! At this point, we hadn't even had pudding! This was horrific. I was so out of my depth. I took a ten-dollar mouthful of fish, "Well you seem rather standoffish..."

Eyes wide, she replied, "Really?! After what I just said to you?" She had a point. "Well, um, fair enough, but you're sat way over there, we could be sitting on the couch or something." She looked directly at me, "Oh I wasn't thinking of the couch!"

Obviously, being British, my expression didn't change, but inside I was thinking, "Oh my goodness! Isn't there going to be any handholding? Looking into each other's eyes? Something? Anything?" Then she said, "I know what we're going to do."

I was relieved, at least one of us knew what we were doing. She continued, "I'll do the dishes, you go upstairs and get ready."

So I did.

I took off my boots and socks and sat on her sheets. They were very expensive apparently, organic. They were made from tree bark. I gingerly took off my shirt so I was now feeling a bit chilly. I didn't really know what else to take off. When she came upstairs I plucked up the courage to ask, "Shall I take anything else off?"

I was now twelve.

She said, "Take everything off."

I slipped between the sheets. She got in beside me. I saw she had the body of a twenty-year-old. Suffice to say, our *love-making* was an act of great athleticism, hers, not mine. I did not feel particularly included. At about two in the morning, she woke me up, "You'll have to go now. I can't sleep with anyone in the bed."

I fumbled around for my clothes in the dark. I thought my days of having to creep out in the middle of the night were over. Apparently not. It was dawning on me: it was going to take courage to be a grown-up lesbian in Hollywood.

I went out with Blair for about two months, but in the end, I was just dating an idea. And possibly her house. I was trying to change her, she was trying to change me. I longed for depth, she longed for Botox. I survived the torture of the pubic landing strip, her celebrity dentist, brutal workouts at the gym. We just weren't compatible. And let's face it, I wasn't over Juliette. I got that uneasy feeling again. I said goodbye.

In the meantime, Juliette had never given up on me as she plotted her escape from France. She said she still loved me and truth be told, I still loved her. I had tried to erase her from my mind. Unsuccessfully.

# CHAPTER THIRTY-ONE

'll always remember the day Juliette arrived in Hollywood at my one-room studio with her eight Louis Vuitton suitcases. We soon moved into an old cabin. It was Rock Hudson's old summerhouse. It had raccoons in the roof. We made it cosy, did yoga, went to auditions, did more yoga. It was an opportunity to make up for precious lost time. She no longer had to look over her shoulder and neither did I. We had a simple life: playing house, ending the day curled up with a glass of wine, watching a movie. It was the life I had always dreamed of. No one was going to come knocking on our door to either separate or shame us. To our closest friends and neighbours we were out, but to the rest of the world we were just friends, oh and on a bad day we were identified as mother and daughter. There were no public displays of affection. Juliette in particular was not wanting to sabotage her movie career. Being a lesbian would be disadvantageous. That was a relief for me. I was yet to feel comfortable being a lesbian in public. On the 'outness' scale, I still preferred to stay in the shadows. Men high up in the industry offered Juliette roles in their films for *arrangements*. The casting couch was alive and well and more sordid than I could have ever imagined. She turned them down but, eventually, a year into our living together, she was pursued by Karl, a big-time producer.

At that time she and I were deep into kundalini yoga teacher training. It was after a two-hour meditation in the backyard that the words, "Are you going to marry Karl?" fatefully fell from my lips. We were both in shock, but her hesitation in answering the question told me everything I needed to know. I continued, "If you want to try him out, you have my blessing but I just may not be here when you come back."

She cried and I cried and we knew it was done. Juliette wanted all the normal things like children and family. I had made it clear that at age fifty, I no longer envisaged having children. That moment had passed me by twenty years earlier and I did not want to be the one to deprive her. Neither of us felt it necessary to leave the beautiful home we had created. After all, there had been no falling out. So she moved into the spare room.

She and Karl lasted two months. Four days after their breakup, she came out of our bathroom holding a pregnancy test. It was positive. We looked at each other.

"Do you want the baby?" I asked.

"Well, of course! I don't want to get rid of it if that's what you mean!"

"Well, congratulations then!" I felt happy for her. We sat down together at the kitchen table.

"I will have to tell Karl," she sighed.

"Do you think you should maybe give it another go, with Karl? He is the baby's father after all." I had gone into the mentor role, which had been my default since the start of the Karl relationship. Now there was a baby on the way and that was really all that mattered.

She told Karl that night about the baby and that she wanted them to start over. He was over the moon.

My mother could not have timed her arrival in L.A. more perfectly! Mother's original response to my telling her about the relationship with Juliette two years earlier had been, "Darling, you promised me that you would never get yourself into this situation again. David and I were very understanding and forgiving about your relationship with Alexandra. And I won't be visiting you in America with this "unpleasantness" going on!"

"Well, if you ever change your mind Mum, you will always be welcome," had been my response.

Pressure from friends and family, as well as finding herself widowed, had resulted in a change of heart. Meeting her at Arrivals at Los Angeles Airport, she admitted to being a little nervous about the difficult situation she was about to walk in to but she couldn't help cracking a smile as I lowered the roof of the Mustang and handed her big shades and silk headscarf, "You're going to need these, Mum."

It thrilled me to see her excitement catching sight of the Hollywood sign way in the distance, "It's such a shame" (she started most of her sentences with this) It's such a shame that you are in this awful situation with this girl."

"Well Mum, I have some news in that department." She bit her lip and looked stonily ahead.

"Juliette and I are still living in the same house but we are no longer a couple. She is now going out with a very nice chap called Karl and she is expecting his baby."

There was a long silence. Mother removed her sunglasses and breathed on them slightly to clean them. As she replaced them she stared directly at the freeway ahead and expressionless, she let out a huge sigh, "Well, I am so relieved, that is such good news darling!" And all was well.

*Fiona Goodwin*

Despite their best efforts, Karl and Juliette were not to be. When Juliette faced her reality, that she could not be with a man, any man, she told him. His situation and heartbreak were such that he felt unable to maintain the long distance connection with Jacques.

The prayer then, and still now, is that that will change and that father and son will one day find each other.

The dilemma I found myself in at this point was considerable. Juliette wanted us to reconcile and to build a family together. She had broken up with Karl because she wanted to be with me. I initially didn't know what to do and then warmed to the idea that maybe this was the child I could never have myself. Mid-pregnancy, I threw myself into parenting classes and broke it to my mother, my poor mother, that yet again my circumstances had changed. I was now going to be a parent. There was an icy silence over the phone, followed a few weeks later in the mail, by a woolly bonnet and matching babygrow. Mother loved babies.

Jacques was born in our sitting room June 3rd, 2007. Music, low lighting candles, a birthing pool, and a Sikh midwife. The centre of my world had shifted. Now I really was in love. With a baby boy.

Mostly I remember that feeling at the LACMA summer concerts, holding him in my arms, swaying to the music, surrounded by families and picnics and tacos and beer.

Our little boy was eight months old when Juliette's visa ran out. She had to go back to France. I couldn't imagine life without Jacques so I said I would go with them. I thought I was ready to leave my American life behind but I had that uneasy feeling, that voice in my gut. I did love our little family, but the Karl situation had taken its toll, and comedy, the reason I had moved to L.A. had been lost. Sometimes that inner voice is the last thing you want to hear. I was fifty-one and with an aching heart, I let them go. Juliette and I remain close, Jacques is now eleven; he has a delightful new other mum. He visits regularly. I've been on the Santa Monica roller coaster a lot. He and I have an unbreakable bond.

*Fiona Goodwin*

# CHAPTER THIRTY-TWO

.........................................

Waking up that first day without them, I felt clear in a way that I hadn't for months The void and the grief were all over me but the torture of the decision about whether to stay or go with them, had gone. So much guilt and dissection: abandoning Juliette to single motherhood and abandoning Jacques who I had briefly called my son, was unspeakably painful. I hadn't been able to think straight. Now I had calm. Not to mention time. All those hours spent taking care of Jacques now needed to be filled. I drove to Santa Fe for Thanksgiving and tried to replace the bouts of desolation with the luxury of being single and unencumbered.

Back in L.A. I dived into the comedy scene and reveled in being able to stay out till the small hours, The Comedy Store, Malo's, Flappers. I was picking up steam. I never sought out lesbians, and nor was my comedy about being gay. I was still in hiding and justified it by telling myself that I didn't want to be identified solely as a lesbian comic. I attended writing classes. I started to formulate the idea of telling my story.

Just as I was starting to get some lift-off, I found out that Mother had been diagnosed with congestive heart failure.

Following my stepfather's passing five years previously, I had visited the UK very briefly for the funeral. I had found it almost impossible to be in the presence of her pain. She was beside herself with grief and beyond comfort of any sort. Certainly from me. She felt abandoned by my leaving for LA so soon, but truthfully she had always felt abandoned. Evacuation from London during the war, age five to ten, had defined her inner landscape. She once, and once only, described lining up for the train at Victoria Station. Operation Pied Piper took her and a thousand other children out of London and away from the danger of the German air raids. Her name and address were tied around her neck with rough string, along with an oversized gas mask. She held her teddy bear under one arm and a child's suitcase in the other. She would see her parents but a handful of times in the following five years. She was terrorized and locked in cupboards for whole nights by the older girls at the catholic boarding school. When she was old enough to write, she sent letters to her parents, begging them to come and get her. Her letters were destroyed by the nuns and her parents never knew. Consequently, when she herself became a mother, she held onto her three children so tight that consciously or unconsciously, we all ended up living at diametrically opposite ends of the globe—Melbourne, Munich, and Los Angeles. She saw betrayal and cruelty in everything we did. In my late teens, at the end of a regular bout of her disappointment and accusations, I sobbed in recognition, "I have spent my entire childhood trying to convince you that I love you and you have never believed me and you never will."

So, that was the backdrop, forty years later for my next decision. I phoned my brothers with the shocking suggestion, "I'm feeling that I should go home to take care of Mother." They were both anxious for me, "Why would you do that? You know that as soon as you get there, she will recover and live for another twenty years and you will be stuck there. The guilt will be too much and you'll never get away."

I couldn't help agreeing with them but the idea would not leave me.

My therapist asked me the question that solidified my decision, "Fiona, if you knew that your mother would recover and would live for another twenty years, would it change how you feel about wanting to go and take care of her now?"

Without hesitation, I answered, "No, it wouldn't. I know it doesn't make sense knowing what I know about my relationship with my mother, but I want to take care of her." I was surprised by my answer and by the deep certainty that I felt in that moment. And so I did. Initially, I got work in London managing a cocktail bar, just visiting mother at weekends and I embarked on completing my credentials as a psychotherapist.

It was the year of the Queen's Diamond Jubilee. Fifty years earlier, aged nineteen, Mother had been at the coronation of the young Queen Elizabeth. She had stood for hours on the Mall, waiting for the carriage to go by. I got it into my head that I wanted her to see the Queen one more time but her breathing was too bad and she said she wouldn't be able to cope with the crowds. I was disappointed but managed to persuade her to join me the day before the celebrations when it would be quiet. It was warm and sunny. I hired a rickshaw from Piccadilly, which daringly dodged the traffic down Pall Mall, Marlborough Rd, and onto the Mall. Mother, though weak and breathless, held on tight and giggled all the way. We were dropped off outside the palace and stood in front of the gates, taking in the grandeur and the memories of times gone by. Rehearsals were going on in preparation for the next day's big event.

"It's such a shame we won't be here tomorrow." I immediately recognized that I had adopted her favourite expression. She came back with, "No, this is perfect." And then the magic happened.

A six-foot machine-gun carrying policeman spoke to mother, "Ma'am, could you please move away from the gates." Mother wasn't having any of it. "Why do we have to move?" The policeman tried again," Ma'am, could you please move away from the gates."

Again she was undeterred, "Why should we, is something going to happen?"

"Ma'am I won't ask again, please move away from the gates," and then in a whisper," and you might want to get your camera out."

Mother and I looked at each other and then back at the policeman. We scuttled to the side of the gates. I reached for my phone just as the huge wrought iron gates swung wide and six motorbike outriders headed towards us from the inside of the palace, followed by a black Bentley with a fluttering royal insignia.

"Oh my God Mum! It's her! It's the Queen!" Mother was expressionless, stunned, almost as if this was an everyday occurrence. She clutched her handbag a little more tightly and fixed her gaze on the approaching cavalcade. As the Bentley swept through the gates, the Queen in the back seat looked directly at us, the only people there, and she smiled. The Queen smiled at us! Tears sprung to my eyes—my dream had become reality! I felt so proud.

The photo marking the occasion was framed and sat by her bed for the few remaining months of her life. I heard later from Mother's friends what a thrill it had been for her. She was unable to express that to me but I had learned by then not to expect that. Maybe she thought that if she appeared happy, I would think she didn't need me and I would abandon her. I was rarely in receipt of her approval.

Mother's decline was more rapid following the encounter with the Queen. It was the beginning of the reversal roles. I moved in with her full-time. At first, she was mobile and could, with help, make it to the lounge room. I washed her and brushed her hair. Sometimes, I would be overcome with gratitude that I could take care of her. However, since I was no longer working, I was running out of money, funding her and her eighty-year-old boyfriend who daily came for lunch. I asked her for help. She responded with, "Darling, you have free rent and board. I think paying for the food is the least you can do."

I was ready for this, "Well Mum, I'll have to get a job and I won't be able to take care of you." She was defiant, "Darling, I will be absolutely fine. If you need to go to work, I can get my own meals, thank you very much. And now you can take me to the bathroom." I didn't argue with her. That would have been pointless. I was perplexed about what to do. She refused to pay for a carer and she refused to use a commode.

Many nights, I found her on the floor, soaked in urine, "Mum, you could have used the buzzer and I would have come down."

"Well darling, I just didn't want to bother you. I was trying to manage on my own."

Very gently I said, "Well Mum, you could have a really bad fall and in actual fact, it would be less of a bother if you asked for help."

She gave me that deeply wounded look, "Don't be like that, you're being mean."

"I don't mean to be mean—what about the commode?"

"I refuse to have that in my room, I will not be reduced to that. If you slept in my room it wouldn't be a problem." That sent a shudder through me, "I would rather sleep in my own room, sorry Mum."

It was a game I couldn't win. I started waking up at 3 a.m. every night anticipating her night manoeuvres, and most nights when I appeared at her door, she would be sitting on the edge of her bed, wide awake, her face would break into a huge smile. She looked about six, "How do you know? How do you know when to come?"

"I don't know mum, I just wake up."

"That's amazing!" I lifted her into the wheelchair and wheeled her to the bathroom, where I would lift her out and have to swing her around in the narrow space, lift her nightie, and put her on the toilet. As she got thinner, that became easier. One night I arrived too late—she was already on the floor in a mess. When I got her to the bathroom, she clung on to me tight and whispered in my ear, "You saved me, you know." I choked back the tears, "Well Mum, you saved me too…you must have cleaned me up a few times!"

"Just a few." She smiled, remembering.

I got her back to her room, she waited in the wheelchair while I changed the sheets. I asked her, as I did every night, "Mum, cup of tea and a biscuit?"

Her face lit up, as if it were the best thing that had ever happened to her and she responded exactly the same every night, "Darling, are you sure you don't mind? Isn't it too much trouble?"

"It's no trouble, Mum. It's fun having tea and biscuits

with you in the middle of the night." And we would sit and chat, nothing deep. As much as she could, she always kept things light and breezy, sipping tea for twenty minutes or so, until her eyes started to droop and I would suggest we get some sleep. She was a small child in those moments. She made me think of the five-year-old who had been sent away for five years and had had no one to put her to bed or sit with her and have tea. I was deeply moved that at the end, I was given the opportunity to do that for her. I no longer felt like the "bad daughter." She eventually did have that fall that I had warned her about. She hated hospitals and pretended for days that she wasn't in pain but she had fractured her pelvis on one of her nighttime expeditions.

At the hospice, she fell in love with the nurses and the morphine. She was there only five days, expecting to return home. I was holding her hand as she struggled to breathe her last. I was crying, "Mum, please don't go," It was unimaginable to me that at the end I wanted more time with her.

At the funeral, I rode in the hearse with the coffin, still not letting go. And somehow it was my way of announcing to the world. "We made it. A truce. The hostility was no more."

I rattled around her house for weeks. It was amazing to sleep through the night. In those final four months, it had just been me and her. She had eventually relented and we had an agency nurse come to get her up and put her to bed. I had visits from friends and family, but it was a deeply intimate and solitary time. I had barely contemplated what I would do when she died. My struggle with her was over. We had divested ourselves of our armour and I was grateful to feel bereft when she passed—my fear had been that I would feel nothing, or worse, relief.

# CHAPTER THIRTY-THREE

The death of Mother was the prelude to the death of hiding. Put another way, I felt a grand permission to do and be whatever I wanted. That somehow translated itself into the wildest escapade of all.

I had overheard the word "ayahuasca" at a social gathering in L.A. People whom I respected had done it. All I knew was that whatever *it* was, it had to be done under supervision. I couldn't get the word "ayahuasca" out of my mind so I googled it. It was a hallucinogenic plant medicine found in the Amazon. It had therapeutic effects, physiological as well as psychological. I liked what I read. The Temple of the Way of Light in Peru had a twelve-day retreat.

Prior to departure, family and friends inundated me with newspaper cuttings of recent ayahuasca-related deaths. Nevertheless, the voice within gave the green light and I put myself on the two-week preparatory diet: no sugar, no animal fat, no dairy, no red meat, almost no salt, no processed food of any kind. I packed the chemical-free mosquito spray (totally ineffective in the Amazon by the way) and the mosquito repellant clothes and took the twelve-hour flight to Lima, two more hours on a smaller plane landed me in Iquitos, the largest town in the world to be accessible only by boat or plane. Following three days of acclimatisation, a bumpy bus ride took me and my fellow *passajeros* to the bank of the River Amazon where we clambered aboard a straw-canopied longboat. We put-putted across the vast stretch of water. It took my breath away, the immensity of it. The other participants seemed surprisingly "unhippy-like," a German doctor, a South African business owner, a Canadian construction worker, a homeopath from the Bronx, a train driver from Newcastle, a translator from the U.N. We were twenty-one in total.

Reaching the other side of the river, we motored another hour along the bank before turning into an opening in the dense jungle. The waterway system became convoluted and narrow. Low hanging vines and branches scraped the sides and roof of the boat. My phone went dead. Excitement turned to fear. I would never be able to find my way home. The jungle valour that I once possessed when I saved the Andrea from the tarantula in Honduras seemed to have evaporated.

Our boatman did not speak English or Spanish. He was a member of the indigenous Shipibo tribe. As we disembarked, tribes people emerged from the undergrowth, and a woman with a toothless smile, half my size and twice my age, tugged at my huge rucksack. She headed off with it at high speed. We tramped for forty minutes in ninety-degree heat through swamps and swarms of mosquitos. At the wooden arch entrance of the compound, there were five women in colourful traditional costumes, standing in line, waiting to welcome us. They were the shamans. Straight shiny black hair with fringes and laughing eyes on wrinkled brown faces. They were tiny. The first one hugged me and said something kind but incomprehensible. My eyes filled with tears, to be here in the Amazon meeting these extraordinary women. It was one of those moments that affirmed my decision to be single. I felt so lucky to have the resources and the freedom from responsibility to make this adventure possible.

The next night, in inky darkness, I drank the dark syrupy liquid and sat waiting to vomit and hallucinate. (The information on the website had played down the purging element of the experience!) The lanterns were extinguished and the screeching and cawing sounds of the jungle reminded me just how far I was from home. My face started to tingle and go numb. My stomach began to churn. It was nine o'clock. The doctor from Germany on the mat next to me heaved into his bucket.

Earlier that day, through a translator, the shamans asked my reason for coming. I didn't know. I told them that I had just kept hearing the word "ayahuasca." They didn't seem surprised and asked to know about my childhood. They nodded wisely and conferred. Their conclusion came back via the translator, "Su corazon es cerrado, her heart is closed. Ayahuasca will open her heart. We like easy cases!" Their impassive, wizened faces gave way to warmth and laughter at my incredulity. Their confidence was infectious.

The medicine finally kicked in. A flood of random images—wicker blinds, a golden light behind them that I longed for but could not reach, clocks and bells and whir-ring sounds. The nausea was building. It was going to come out of both ends so I staggered to my feet and out of the hut to the bathroom, which was a bucket of sawdust. A tribesman with a shotgun accompanied me. He and five others patrolled the area, guarding us from snakes and black panthers. As I sat there, the toilet paper holder turned into a giant potato and then a rapidly expanding planet. I got fixated on the planet, I had no sense of the passing of time. There was no electricity and my torch became a rocket heading towards outer space. My absence was noticed and a shaman came to rescue me from my reverie and I was escorted back to my mat.

That's when I noticed the staring—men in black goggles: Nazis.

I sensed the weight of the atrocities they had committed. I was terrified but there was no escaping their malevolence. What were they going to do to me? By this time I could hardly move, my body was heavy and sluggish, there was no escaping. I wanted to go home.

A shaman again came to my aid, it was too dark to see her but she started singing in a high-pitched voice. The nausea built up more strongly until I had to quickly reach for my bucket and throw up. The Nazis faded away along with the terror. I was weak and lonely. I finally dozed off and slept deeply in the hut with everyone else till around 6 a.m.

Later that morning, we compared notes: a thirty-year-old Spanish woman who had been chronically depressed for five years felt absolutely nothing. The Canadian construction worker was agitated and fretful. The Newcastle train driver was in complete bliss.

I garbled on about the Nazis, "They were glaring at me. It was horrific," and then came the epiphany, "It was how my mother used to look at me." My eyes filled with tears, it was making sense, my new companions nodded their heads in recognition. The hallucination was a representation of the terror of childhood.

On the third ceremony, I was tiring of trying to make sense of the Sergeant Pepper-like images, the complex yellow structures, wormholes, and tunnels. It all felt meaningless. I found myself wondering again, "How is this helping me to open my heart?"

Then I saw him—my father.

He was standing at the end of a hallway. It was our old house. He was in his late twenties, wearing grey slacks and a grey wool sweater. He was looking back at me, weeping. He was holding open the front door and from behind him, a bright light was pouring into the passageway. He came back to me and picked me up and I felt the familiar sensation of his wool sweater rough against my cheek. He explained that he was leaving, that he didn't want to go but he couldn't stay. I was engulfed in grief, *his* grief for the loss of his children. I begged him, "Please don't go! You are breaking up my family." The crying turned to deep sobs, I was again engulfed in the loss, his and mine. I felt the depth of his love for the very first time.

The grieving would die down but when I thought there could be no more, there would be another wave. At times, it was too deep to even make a sound. During the hallucination of the sixth night, I was confronted by a fifteen-foot anaconda. I knew it was going to swallow me. I waited for certain death and then its left eye closed, it winked at me!

"Are you a friendly snake?" I asked.

"Yes," it replied and I felt its warmth.

"So, can I call you Snakey Snake?"

Again it replied, "Yes." I thought some more, "What are you here for?"

"Let me show you," was its reply, "follow me."

It slithered into my childhood bedroom back to the scene of my father's departure. I watched as it wrapped itself around my wracked little child's body and I felt heat, physical heat. It explained, "I was there all the time, I saw everything. I can heal you retrospectively."

On my mat, I felt held and soothed in a way I had never

felt before. Snakey Snake spoke again, not in actual words but in silent transmissions, "I was always there and I will never leave you."

The next morning, I felt Snakey Snake still there and the aloneness had gone. I mused, "This is what it must feel like to be in a real couple, like someone always has your back."

The culmination of the ayahuasca experience was the hallucination of the final ceremony. I found myself sitting on Mother's hospital bed at home. We were having our usual cosy cup of tea at three in the morning when I asked her," Mum, what was it like to die?"

She responded very matter-of-factly, "It wasn't as bad as I thought, darling. You see, I thought I would die alone... I never knew I had this daughter."

Those words have never left me, the antithesis of what I had experienced when she was alive. I was hearing what I had always wanted to hear, her recognition of who I really was. She had finally discovered me—our late-night skirmishes to the bathroom, cleaning her up when I found her soaked in urine. I wanted to know more, "Was there anything else I could have done for you?"

She answered in her upper-crust manner, "Yes darling there was, you could have smartened yourself up, you were always wearing that shabby dressing gown." I laughed. She was right, sheer exhaustion meant that I rarely bothered to get dressed.

Those bizarre conversations facilitated by the ayahuasca significantly healed that difficult relationship. That was the reason I had come to Peru. I left a huge weight of grief there. My heart had indeed been opened, to my mother, to my father, and to myself. It was as if I had been rebooted, I was ready for the next chapter.

# CHAPTER THIRTY-FOUR

Returning to the empty house in England and mother's belongings still intact was like going back in time, but the journey up the Amazon River had created closure. There was no longer that heaviness of loss. I had a new relationship with Mother. She was gone, but my heart was now fully open to her. By accessing my own kindness in caring for her, I had opened a door of kindness for myself. I was less alone.

This was the true exorcism that I had been praying for, forever. The exorcism of isolation and rejection. In the end, I had not failed as a daughter. At the time of the decision to care for Mother, I had no concept of the breadth of its reach. With every cup of tea and every time I scooped her up off the floor, I was pouring salve on my own shame and self-hatred. My surrendering to her loaded silence around my sexuality led to a surrender in my inner landscape. The shame of the "bad gay daughter" who never found love with a man, who never wore pretty dresses, who never provided grandchildren, and who, out of fear, abdicated her own desires. That daughter came home to herself and found peace.

I wondered what to do next. I slowly realised what my heart was calling me to do. It was inviting me to tell the story, to put my adventures into words. For some undeniable reason, that had to happen in California, where I had first found acceptance.

So that's what I did. I returned to the sunshine, the comedy clubs, and too much yoga. It was the land of *you can do and be whatever you want.* I had a newfound audacity. It was time to tell my story on stage. I hired a director and wrote and wrote. I remembered the childhood loneliness, the dawning horror of being gay, the failed exorcism, the homage to Julie Andrews in Italy, the passion in the jungles of Honduras, my forays into the worlds of wild salmon and tame men, the love and loss of Alexandra and her family, and finally my brief encounter with motherhood. Mostly I remembered the hiding, the decades of not being truthful or true to who I was. I hadn't wanted to go to hell, not the one in life, or the one in the afterlife. All the while I had continually told myself that if I just had enough therapy, I would "straighten out." In the end, I was being reacquainted with my favourite adage, "You shall know the truth and the truth will set you free."

All of these events, as if by some invisible hand, had conspired to liberate me, to strengthen my own voice. The show was written and I was invited to put it into a festival. I was excited but the nearer it got to the entry deadline, the more frightened I became. I phoned my director, "I can't do it, and I can't have the word 'lesbian' in the title."

A no-nonsense New Yorker, she laughed, "Well, it's kinda what the show's about, so messing with the title, really isn't going to help you a whole lot."

I managed to raise a weak smile, "Well, I feel sick and no one is going to want to see a show about a lesbian." I said the word "lesbian" as I always did, with disdain.

"Well, you have two days left to decide, and maybe you

should think about why, and who you wrote this show for. Get back to me."

I did think about it, all day and all night. I was a lesbian. There was no getting away from that. I had, after all, continued to date women but still there was the shame, the wondering what people would think.

And then, the following night, still undecided, I was watching the news. It was the night of the massacre at Pulse, the Orlando gay nightclub—forty-nine people gunned down. They had been dancing! Dancing! I felt rage at the homophobia. Especially my own.

The next day, I was walking with my new girlfriend, on the Santa Monica Pier. We were surrounded by crowds and rainbow flags and outrage. I knew what I had to do. The voice that had guided me to next, the voice that took me to God, that led me away from the convent, that insisted I fall in love with women, that coaxed me out of the smallness of being the third wheel, that brought me to California, to a beautiful young woman and a baby boy. That same voice was telling me to come out of hiding, really come out of hiding. So, with the whole world watching, I took my girlfriend's hand and we walked together hand in hand, for everyone to see. Being unashamed, being authentic, being gloriously myself, produced a rush of adrenalin that was other-worldly. I wanted more!

"Excuse me," I told my girlfriend, "I have to make a quick call." I took out my phone and called the director, "It's on, we're doing it…"

"Good," she said, "and the title?"

Without hesitating, I said, "What we agreed."

"Even better, see you tomorrow at the theatre."

*Fiona Goodwin*

# CHAPTER THIRTY FIVE

I was staring into the dressing room mirror of the Santa Monica Playhouse, when the stage manager popped her head in the door, "Fiona, this is your one-minute call. Break a leg!" Heart pounding, I stood up and headed for the wings. The house lights went down, the music went up and I walked out on stage to be greeted by a roar of applause. I looked at the sea of smiling faces staring back at me. I stood tall, took a deep breath and smiled back,

"Good evening, ladies and gentlemen. I'm Fiona Goodwin—and I am A Very British Lesbian."

# ACKNOWLEDGEMENTS

My sincere thanks go to:

My high school students - thank you for twenty-one years of friendship and daily opportunities for stand-up!

Kat Waring, for making me run a lot and the tattoo!

Lucy Garnier, for making me seem clever, and for the Red Book - I still have it!

Susi Elton née Schofield - for being my right hand woman in our work with adolescents and for carrying the torch of emotional literacy. Your humanity is God sent.

The Christians - for being so loving and well-intentioned. Thank you especially to those who remained friends despite my failed exorcisms!

Judith Ptaszyinski, my oldest friend, for surviving my teenage self and for always being a port in the storm.

The Willing family - Kate, Matthew, James, Wendy, Jennifer, Michael, Hannah (Coetzee) You might not be in the book, but you're such an important part of the story. Such adventures and inappropriate laughter..!

James Barrett UK - Jungian Psychoanalytic Psychotherapist - you opened the door to the joy of analysis.

Robert Razz (RIP) - Insight Seminar facilitator - for showing me the power of vulnerability. I miss you.

Stephen Islas - Spiritual Counsellor- for ushering me into

my American life and for teaching me that the truth will never cheat you.

Natasha Wood - Actress/Producer/Writer/Comedian, for fresh trout at Granville's and your unfailing support of all my endeavours: comedic, artistic and romantic!

Gavin Frye - Psychotherapist L.A. - for so much friendship and fearlessly guiding me to bigger and bigger risks of the heart.

Sally Ingram - Psychotherapist BACP - for friendship and for encouraging me to become an accredited member of the British Association of Counsellors and Psychotherapists.

Drs. Ron and Mary Hulnick and the University of Santa Monica, for the path to self-acceptance and the permission to dream.

Laurel Airica - Poet extraordinaire and most loyal friend - for opening up your home, for your brilliant insight and unwavering support, for your unceasing quest for truth and WordMagic!

Maria Gobetti - Acting Coach Hollywood - for Meisner technique, for telling me to write, for a beautiful Christmas Eve at your home, for supporting me when I lost my way and my mind!

Holland Taylor - Actress - for your generous encouragement in my pursuit of comedy.

Susan & Kevin Dobson - Producer/Actor - thank you for opening your doors to me when I needed a place to stay and Susan for taking me to the House of Blues that auspicious night when I got my foot in the door.

Terrie Silverman - Writing teacher - thank you for your inspirational classes, for helping me to get on my comedy feet, for driving miles to my first paid gig.

The Twelve Step programmes (plural!) too numerous to mention! Thank you Bill!

Nadia Angelini - Intuitive Counsellor/Actress/Musician, for seeing my future and telling me it was good! You were right!

John Daly RIP - Oscar-winning film producer - for so kindly giving me my unlikely break in Hollywood.

Jett Kearney for opening my heart wider than I ever thought possible.

Sarah Kearney - Actress/Australian Midwife, for our magical life together in Hollywood, for sharing your beautiful son, for introducing me to oysters and champagne, for supporting my American dream, for never giving up on your own.

Simonne Lee - Life Coach/Animal Communicator - for understanding my challenges and the challenges being faced by my friends' cats.

Kacie Stetson - Actress/Acting Coach NZ, for introducing me to the New York Film Academy, Los Angeles where the fun started!

Benedicta and Geoffry Oblath - Writer/Lawyer, for supporting my writing, for the best roast beef this side of the Atlantic!

John Cairns - Parkland Pictures - Film Producer/Distributor, for Vegas with my mother, for sushi in Santa Monica, for sharing our home in Hollywood, for giving me a job managing your restaurant/cocktail bar in London. You're more fun than should be allowed!

Russell Carpenter - Oscar-winning Cinematographer - Titanic. Thank you for picking me up when I was sinking, and for making me look good!

Mia Korf - Actress - and daughter Matea Korf, for endless late night cups of tea, for adopting me and making me go to comedy school. For opening so many doors! I miss you!

Comedian Adam Barnhardt's comedy workshops and for getting me my first gig at The Comedy Store.

Jeannine Brousseau - Hollywood Hair Stylist, for being a genius at what you do - both with hair and with hearts.

Mhairi Morrison - Actress/Voice Over Artist/Activist - for making the Hollywood comedy circuit more fun and funnier than it would have been! And for sharing your relationship with Jamie Oliver!

The Amazonian Shipibo tribe - for the healing work of ayahuasca.

Mary Jane Wells - Actress/Writer/Voice Over Artist/Activist, for your bottomless generosity sharing your expertise in all things show biz.

Paul Duddridge - Entertainment Coach - for tirelessly liberating me from my inauthenticity - your impact continues to be profound. I don't think any of this would have happened without you.

Hollywood Acting Coach, Margie Haber and her wife Susan, for deep talk, dinners and for going above and beyond - you know what I mean!

Actress/Comedian/faithful friend - Wendy Hammers, for being an inspirational dramaturge and brilliant director of

"A Very British Lesbian."

J Patrick Carroll - Shamanic Recovery, for your depth of work and generosity.

Michael Blaha - Entertainment Lawyer/Producer, for so valiantly fighting for the show at the Edinburgh Fringe Festival.

Kate Copstick - Actress/Producer/Critic/Writer for coming to see *A Very British Lesbian* when you didn't have to and for your wonderful review.

Melanie Mayron - Actress/Director/Producer, for your support, and for giving me the Thanksgiving turkey carcass to take home - soup for weeks!

Comedian/Activist Robin Tyler - the original LGBTQ pioneer - for feeding me, for the swimming pool and for your amazing support of the show.

Susan and Darry Sragow - for your friendship, political education (you tried at least!) and regular supply of chicken wings.

James Milhaley - Writing Coach - for labouring alongside me in the birthing of this book. I would have given up without your unique combination of sensitivity and insistence.

Mehret Mehary - International Financier and neighbour, thank you for your delicious and joyful Ethiopian hospitality and that your door and heart are always open.

Andrea Meyerson - Award winning Producer/Director - and lesbian supporter - Women on the Net - thank you for opening the door to Provincetown.

Shaman Sumi Sung - for continuing to restore my connection to the Divine.

My psychotherapy clients for your love and courage and for the privilege of walking beside you.

Keith Goodwin - thank you Dad for sharing your love of fast cars!

Beverly Clarke - Spears Travels - for literally saving my mother's life on more than one occasion and for saving mine after she passed away. Best neighbour ever!

David Kwak - friend and finder of fast cars - for your kindness and the Jaguar XK8 with cream leather seats and walnut dashboard.

Faith Finch - thank you Mum for passing on to me the performance gene...and a love of heart shaped cake.

David Finch - thank you for being Mother's rock.

My brothers Christopher Goodwin and Rupert Finch - for making it okay to emigrate! Thank you for supporting my dreams and being proud of me.

"Corona Live Poetry Left Coast Lesbian Lunch Crying in Bed with Fiona Show" and the Fionians - thank you for rescuing me during Covid and for letting me know that you wanted to read the book, making it imperative to finish it!

For those dear to my heart who cannot be mentioned for reasons of confidentiality, I hope you know who you are - I am forever grateful.

Finally In the words of Julio Iglesias, "To all the girls I've loved before." Forgive me for having been so frightened of going to Hell!

No longer!!!